What Every English Teacher Should Know

By
J. N. Hook
Paul H. Jacobs
Raymond D. Crisp

What Every English Teacher Should Know

By
J. N. Hook
Paul H. Jacobs
Raymond D. Crisp

A publication of the Illinois State-Wide Curriculum Study Center in the Preparation of Secondary School English Teachers (ISCPET)

Consultant Readers

DOUGLAS C. CAMPBELL, Santa Rosa (California) High School District

PAUL T. ROSEWELL, MacMurray College

NCTE Committee on Publications

ROBERT F. HOGAN, NCTE Executive Secretary, Chairman

CHARLOTTE S. HUCK, Ohio State University

HENRY W. SAMS, Pennsylvania State University

MILDRED W. WEBSTER, St. Joseph (Michigan) Senior High School

EUGENE C. ROSS, NCTE Director of Publications

Editorial Services

CYNTHIA H. SMITH, NCTE Headquarters

Book Design

NORMA PHILLIPS, NCTE Headquarters

Library of Congress Catalog Card Number 72-101529
Standard Book Number 8141-2111-2
NCTE Stock Number 21112

Table of Contents

Preface   vi

Once There Was a Child . . .   x

. . . And a Teacher   xvi

1. Knowledge of Language   1

2. Knowledge and Skill in Written Composition
(Imaginative and Expository)   17

3. Knowledge and Skill in Literature   37

4. Knowledge and Skill in Oral Communication   53

5. Knowledge and Skill in the Teaching of English   65

Appendix A. ISCPET Institutional Representatives and
Conductors of Special Studies   79

Appendix B. Special Studies Conducted by ISCPET   83

Preface

This book is intended for three kinds of readers. First, it is addressed to the prospective teacher of English, especially in the secondary schools. It should preferably be put into the hands of that teacher-to-be while he is still a college freshman or sophomore, so that he can more intelligently elect courses and can understand why certain courses in a well-conceived program are required. It can be a useful guide throughout his college career.

Second, the book is addressed to the experienced teacher of English, to whom it may suggest his areas of greatest need for postgraduate work, private reading, and other inservice education, and to the high school or college department chairman, who will find it helpful for inservice planning.

Third, it is intended for those college professors responsible for curricular planning in preparation of secondary school English teachers. Such professors may find suggestions which, if incorporated into the programs for which they are responsible, will add strength.

This is not a methods text. It is not intended to tell anyone how to teach or, except in passing, what to teach. The book is no more and no less than the reasoned statement suggested by the title: *What Every English Teacher Should Know*. Other books and other experiences must be relied on to provide answers to questions about methodology and specific content.

The book is based upon a five-year study conducted in Illinois. In 1964 twenty Illinois colleges and universities began a cooperative venture intended to seek ways to improve the preparation of secondary school teachers of English. The acronym ISCPET is used to designate this Illinois State-Wide Curriculum Study Center in the Preparation of Secondary School English Teachers. Armed with funds from the U.S. Office of Education plus additional contributions from the member colleges, mainly in released time, the twenty institutions embarked on their five-year study, with representatives of English and education working together.

What Every English Teacher Should Know represents part of the harvest from five years of ISCPET work. Yet it is not a summary in the sense that the official ISCPET final report is a summary. Rather, it is a distillate of information and beliefs born or reinforced during the study, and it draws upon non-ISCPET sources as freely as it does upon ISCPET. This book is only one of many products of the Center's work. More than thirty special studies, conducted by faculty members of the twenty institutions, have made a systematic attack on a number of problems facing colleges that prepare teachers, and many of their conclusions are incorporated implicitly in this book. The complete list of special studies and their directors is given in the appendices.

Shortly after ISCPET began, the representatives conferred with their Advisory Committee, with secondary teachers and department heads, and with administrators and certification specialists and then, drawing upon these conferences and upon their own knowledge and reading, drew up a document called "Qualifications of Secondary School Teachers of English: A Preliminary Statement." This statement was published in *College English* in November 1965 and about thirty thousand reprints of it have been distributed. It has stood up well, although the final statement reflects some changes in substance and emphasis. It describes in outline form "minimal," "good," and "superior" qualifications in language, literature, written composition, oral composition, and the teaching of English. It is reproduced in five parts in this book, at the beginnings of chapters 1-5, and provides the basic structure for those chapters.

Though all ISCPET institutions are located in Illinois, the special studies, the Qualifications statement, and this book are addressed to a national audience. The ISCPET representatives considered their Center a pilot project that could benefit the entire nation.

The indebtedness of the authors extends to many persons cooperating in the work of ISCPET: the institutional representatives and conductors of special studies, the Advisory Committee, ad hoc committees within the cooperating institutions, the ISCPET Executive Committee, speakers and consultants, and, in particular, the headquarters staff. Their names and institutions appear in Appendix A and can only be listed with blanket thanks for their varied contributions.

A special debt is due to personnel within the U.S. Office of Education and to the deans and department heads and professors in the twenty institutions who, though not always directly involved in ISCPET, gave the project their continued blessing, interest, and support. The authors are particularly grateful to University of Illinois Dean Robert W. Rogers of the College of Liberal Arts and Sciences, Dean Rupert Evans of the College of Education, Professor A. Lynn Altenbernd as English Department head, and Mrs. Mary Katherine Peer, the English Department secretary who solved many of our problems.

J.N.H.
P.H.J.
R.D.C.

Once There Was a Child...

Once a child was born. In the same minute, about six other children were born in the United States; in the same hour four hundred and fifty; in the same day about eleven thousand; in the same year four million.

The child's skin was called black, or white, or brown, or yellow, or red. The color shouldn't have made any difference, but it did.

The child had parents and grandparents and great-grandparents and great-great-grandparents (though he perhaps knew only one of them or two of them or none of them). And his body and his mind, his questions, his slowness, his smile, his frown, his gaiety, his somberness—all depended in some measure upon fortuity, upon who his parents and grandparents to the dim beginnings were, upon a chance engagement of genes. A random mating in a cave, a thousand almost random matings millenniums ago contributed uniqueness to this body, to this mind. The fortuitousness of ancestry, of heredity, of gene-mingling, shouldn't have made any difference, but it did.

The child was born in a place. The place was a grimy city, a scrubbed suburb, a somnolent small town, a farm with white buildings and white fences, or grey buildings and limp, rusty fences. The place was South, North, East, or West. Geographic accident shouldn't have made any difference, but it did.

A roof was over the child's head, unless he was especially unlucky or lucky. Some roofs sag, disheartened but not ready to give up. Most are trim and straight. Roofs are curtains against the sky. And they conceal. What do the roofs and the walls hide? What love, what cruelty; what wisdom, what folly; what phrasings, what inarticulateness; what hope, what hopelessness? The roofs, the walls conceal. What was under the roofs shouldn't have made any difference, but it did.

And the child was alone and the child was not alone, and from his aloneness he learned and from his not-aloneness he may have learned more. Whitman knew what notaloneness does:

There was a child went forth every day,
And the first object he look'd upon, that object he became,
And that object became part of him for the day or a certain part of the day,
Or for many years or stretching cycles of years . . .
And the friendly boys that pass'd, and the quarrelsome boys,
And the tidy and fresh-cheek'd girls, and the barefoot negro boy and girl,
And all the changes of city and country wherever he went. . . . they became part of him.
The blow, the quick loud word, the tight bargain, the crafty lure . . .
The doubts of day-time and the doubts of night-time, the curious whether and how,
Whether that which appears so is so, or is it all flashes and specks?
These became part of that child who went forth every day, and who now goes, and will always go forth every day.

The child grew, as children have always grown. In all always all ways there is a being and there is a becoming. Yesterday's becoming is today's being. The child's becomings and his

beings were determined by the color of his skin, by random matings in a cave, by a place, by what was under the curtain against the sky, by his daily goings-forth.

Once there was a child who like most children lived sufficiently long that other former children, now grown old and supposedly wise, decided that he had enough years to go to another place, called a school. The former children lived in the nation's capital, and the state capital, and the county seat, and a place called a school board office. They were very old and very supposedly wise former children; and they said, "This child may now go to school."

We teachers need to know more than most of us do. We need especially to know more about children than most of us do, so that, when each child comes to us in this place called a school, we can help him to become the utmost that he is capable of becoming. We do not always do that.

A black boy in a Michigan school was one of the leaders of his class, competing successfully not only with other black students but also with white students from more favored environments. His grades were high and he was a leader in student affairs. He went to talk with his English teacher, who was among those who gave him high grades, to ask him for advice about becoming a lawyer, because he believed, and rightly, that he had enough ability to succeed in law. But the teacher did not help him. He discouraged him from proceeding, suggesting that because he was black he would have a much better opportunity if he enrolled in a trade school and learned carpentry.

This black boy in later years was known as Malcolm X.

But we are talking not only about black boys, or black girls, or Mexican-Americans, or the Puerto Ricans, or the sad remnants of the red race, or the whites who live impoverished in Appalachia and elsewhere. We are talking about the education of all children.

The Fates—or call them God—write that one child lives for hours and another for a century and most for their several decades and then return to non-becoming and nonbeing. The meaning of life, the secret of life, the purpose or nonpurpose of life is encompassed in those countable hours, those too countable years.

Never more time. More of everything else, but never more time. Each child rides in the unknown dimensions of his own time capsule.

Some choose or are influenced to lie almost inert, vegetative as the years pass. Some reach out their hands and grasp other hands and travel quietly through time together. Some spurt ahead, restless, seeking, fervent with adventure, compressing much more than others into each hour and day and year.

What should the teacher know about his work with the time capsules before him? That he cannot wave wands. That he cannot undo the random matings in a cave millenniums ago, nor transmute under-the-rooftops dark secrets, nor always exchange a more society-approved idol for the one on which society frowns, nor force the goings-forth into the paths the teacher himself would like followed. That he cannot roll aside age-old and firmly set boulders, cannot rewrite and reverse history, cannot alter heredity, cannot change Inert Vegetable into Fervent Animal, cannot bodily pick up Two-Miles-Behind and place him in the forefront. The impossible does not, despite the Marines, take just a little longer; the impossible is by definition not possible. And there is no point in beating out one's brains and thrashing sleepless in one's bed because one cannot successfully wave wands and create Utopia.

But the teacher can open vistas.

That is really the function. The teacher is a travel guide, a travel agent. Low-pressure or high-pressure. Both can succeed. He finds out where the children have been and has them show pictures of where they have been. They talk of what they know, and he talks and shows pictures of what he knows; and if they like him and aren't too inhibited, they ask questions about what he knows. They learn from him and from one another. They push ajar a gate that they have been through, and others glimpse what they have never seen before. The willing ones the teacher takes by the hand and leads through the gate; the others have at least had their glimpse and may (some of them) follow later—or some other gate may have more appeal to them. The teacher and the class are constantly opening doors, pushing gates, showing paths and far-off mountains. There are endless realms to explore, and no one can explore them all, because his time capsule is composed of years, and years end.

And always the teacher is aware and helps the children to become aware that beyond the known is a greater unknown. Something lies behind the mountains, and no one has been there. Perhaps there are rich valleys or more mountains, and beyond those valleys or mountains is something else. "Let us move toward the first mountains. Let the more daring some day seek the pass to whatever is beyond. There can be Lewises and Clarks in the twentieth cer ury. Let us look through many gates and see what we can glimpse and decide where we want to move further."

Some children are too crippled to pass through the gates. Some are merely nearsighted and cannot see the first chain of mountains. Even the cripples may have their lives enriched by through-the-gate glimpses of a larger world, even though they can never enter and pick its flowers and swim its streams and dig out its gold. The nearsighted can be fitted with glasses.

Schools exist because children exist. Children are, and are becoming. Schools—elementary, secondary, or collegiate—must accept the being and assist the becoming. The purpose of the schools is to provide choices among all the possible becomings. The people at the Hunter College curriculum study center in New York knew that the severest limitation on their disadvantaged was a limitation of choice. Many children whom they wanted to serve had never been more than two miles from home. *Gateway English* is the title chosen by the Hunter College Center for its printed materials. Opening gates, revealing vistas. How can a child dream if he has nothing to dream about? If he has seen only broken city streets, what can he know of Kansas wheatfields and snow-laden Mount McKinley and islands protruding above ceaseless waves? And if he has never thought beyond the routines of family life and street gangs and dull hours in a grimy school, how can a child's philosophy reach toward "more things in heaven and earth"?

The word *each* is one of the most important in the English language. Each child is different from every other child. Each has his own heredity, ability, acquired knowledge, and potential when he comes into the teacher's classroom. Each can progress only to his own limits, but even the barely "educable," yes, even the barely "trainable," can move some distance ahead, can see something he has not seen before, do something he has not done before. Each teacher helps each child to develop according to his eachness, crawling or plodding or sprinting. "All service ranks the same with God." And if Karl Marx may be quoted out of context and cheek by jowl with Robert Browning,

"From each according to his abilities, to each according to his needs." Or for James Russell Lowell's "kindred" read "person":

Slowly the Bible of the race is writ,
And not on paper leaves nor leaves of stone;
Each age, each [person], adds a verse to it,
Texts of despair or hope, of joy or moan.

No teacher can know too much about children—or enough. But it is possible to learn a great deal, and every teacher learns a little more every day.

College courses can help, though too many are laced with inconsequentials and founded and foundering on a professor's idiosyncrasies. (Professors are human, too. They are not supermen. Sometimes only the raised platform makes them tall.) General psychology, child psychology, and educational psychology can teach much about the child unless they are reduced to memorization of tables and technical terms; when they are, the would-be teacher must often translate for himself a table into a child, a pigeon into a person.

Courses in social psychology and sociology and anthropology can help, too. The child mingles with other children, meets his world, reacts to social forces. The professors, the researchers have generalized the principles of interaction, of human encounters with humanity. Maybe little Joe in your room doesn't behave as the charts say people usually behave; in fact, probably no one in your room does so consistently, but the great Law of Averages prevails and describes a norm that we need to know to understand the abnorm, the offnorm, Little Joe and Big Josephine.

The English teacher is luckier than most other teachers, for his books, his literature courses, can teach him much about children. Not all literature is reliable: Shakespeare's children, such as the impossibly precocious small son of Macduff, are notoriously unrealistic. But there are the children of Mark Twain, and Harper Lee, and John Knowles, and William Golding, and James T. Farrell, and Richard Wright, and E. E. Cummings, and . . . you can extend the list. Literature written especially for children and for adolescents is today much better than it used to be; Pollyanna she dead. A teacher can learn a great deal about the wellsprings of action of today's children by dipping frequently into this wide and sometimes deep pool.

Besides courses and reading, there's observation. See a child. See children. The would-be teacher with younger brothers and sisters is fortunate, unless he generalizes too much on the basis of his own family. The camp counselor sees children minus the inhibitions imposed by the four-walled classroom. The would-be teacher in junior high should see also the fifth grade and the twelfth grade so that he may know what his children were and will be. And in Utopia the college teacher has visited classes in the elementary and high schools, to reduce his myopia and astigmatism.

Perhaps the greatest adventure in

learning to teach is learning about children.

In nature's infinite book of secrecy
A little I can read.

And infinite variety. No two children alike. Each with somewhere to go in his time capsule. Each interacting with each on the journey. Each an enigma, but each shaped and bound by forces he did not create and can change only minutely. Each a contributor in his own way to the inexorable march of humanity toward the great question mark.

...and a Teacher

She glared at the culprit. "By *this* time, George, you certainly ought to know what parentheses mean in a phrase structure rule." George stared at his desk. Tomorrow he would be sixteen, could leave school at any time. Maybe he'd leave tomorrow, though his mother would raise hell. Get a good job—somewhere. Thumb his nose at the goddam school and the goddam teacher and her phrase structure rules. What did they have to do with *him* anyway? He wasn't gonna be no grammarian. He oughta tell her to take her parentheses and stick 'em. Tomorrow he'd be a free man. And someday he'd ride past the school in a big car and yell up toward the windows of Room 322A, "Stick 'em!"

Others in the room, of course, knew about parentheses in phrase structure rules, and she turned sweetly to them and got the answers she wanted. Teachers love the amenable.

Teachers contribute to the dropout rate—and the retention rate. Dropouts are generally those who hate school. Those who stay generally like school. It's not quite so simple as that, for part of the explanation lies in what happens under the rooftops and on the streets, lies even in what happened in the cave a few thousand years ago. But the dropout rate, a symptom of "death at an early age," is usually lowest in those schools where learning, to use the jargon, is "a meaningful experience." That obviously makes the retention rate higher—more kids stick around longer to have more gates pushed ajar for them.

Who is the good teacher of English? What is he? (We'd like to say *he-she* to cope with a weakness of the English language, but *he-she* sounds like what high school boys call a "morphodite.")

Once he lived in a room where he could hear rats scraping and pattering inside the walls, and a sharp nose sometimes appeared where the plaster was broken, and sometimes at night there was a pound of rat crawling and pausing on his body covered, head and all, by soiled sheets and ragged quilt. Somewhere a child cried in hunger or fear. If he looked through the dirty window glass, he could see drunks stumbling in the dim alley, people and dogs and cats scavenging in lidless garbage cans, now and then a savage beating. And in the walls the rats scraped, noisier.

Once he lived in a very different room, a bright immaculate room with books and music and color TV. And he could go into the immaculate kitchen and get a snack from the immaculate refrigerator and walk into what realtors call "a spacious living room," filled with conversation pieces from England and France and Japan, and there he could converse with his well-informed family and friends, not about the conversation pieces but about politics, literature, art, music, education—wherever their fancy led.

He started reading early and at least at times read voraciously. Not always "literature" that his own teachers would have approved. Often westerns and science fiction and detective stories and "true romances" and *Seventeen* and *Good Housekeeping* and Edgar A. Guest and Robert Service and *Playboy* and magazines girlier than *Playboy*. In more serious hours, the *National Geographic, Newsweek,* hobby magazines, and a dozen books on something that attracted him, like geology or astronomy or the stock market.

He read much "literature," too, of course—not just what his teachers assigned. He had favorites whom he tried to read *in toto*—maybe Shakespeare, O'Neill, Hemingway, Cummings, Frost. He found Spenser a little boring but delighted in the portraits and the ribaldries of Chaucer.

As a very young child, he liked to write, and wrote voluntarily. Often "poetry" at first—he loved the tinkle of words and often made meaning subserve rhyme. He started a novel or two or some other vast literary endeavor before he was twelve but never completed it. In high school, if he liked his English teacher, he showed him some of his unassignments. As an adult he still writes, though his expectations of writing the Great American Novel have been reduced.

Before he went to school, he memorized pages of the cheerful gabble of Dr. Seuss from hearing them read to him. Language play fascinated him; he sang a song comprised solely of what to him were the nonsense syllables "vertical stability." Soon he rhymed and punned execrably and riddled endlessly. The love of language and language play never left him.

Almost grown, he walked the streets, alone or in company, peering in windows of shops where he had no intent to buy, watching a tall building under construction, observing people, listening to them, learning the rhythms of multifarious American speech. Curiosity was his mark when he was young, and curiosity remained his mark as the years sped past. He shared what the late Professor Ernest Bernbaum called "the professorial passion for omniscience," knowing that omniscience is unattainable, but curious about everything from how an elevator operates to how hybrid corn is produced.

He knew the countryside, too. As George Henry of Delaware once said about teaching "L'Allegro" and "Il Penseroso," "I never consciously think about teaching Milton from one year to the next; but I do tramp the meadows a great deal and spend a night in a haycock at times, and hunt old forges and charcoal furnaces and colonial farms with 'antique pillars massyproof.'" It is awfully important to be able

To see the world in a grain of sand,
And a heaven in a wild flower.

As a child he quarreled or fought sometimes with his classmates; in fact he did almost everything that the others did (though he had his hours alone, too). He fell in love early and often; he had his childhood crushes and then went through the period when it is *de rigueur* to ignore the other sex, and then he had his first date and in high school he went steady—several times—and in college he was in love and out and went on a few wild parties and was in love and out again.

Once he saw muggers attack a helpless woman. Often he heard disparaging remarks about "kikes," "wops," "niggers," "slant-eyes," "whitey"; and sometimes instead of words there were deeds of discrimination, intimidation, cruelty. He read about assassinations and mourned the deaths. A friend of his who piloted a helicopter was shot down in Vietnam; always, it seemed, a war raged somewhere. Constantly the evidence mounted that man is indeed inhumane to man.

All these experiences helped to make him a good teacher. They helped him to understand literature. More important, they helped him to understand children. Almost regardless of what came up in the classroom, he could say to himself, "I've been there. Something like this has happened to me. I've felt this way myself. I have seen the like. I have struggled, too, through a dark night. I have seen my world collapse. I have foreseen the world ending for me, only to start again." And when, as occasionally happened, a book or a child offered something new, he could say to himself, "Splendid! That's something I didn't know, haven't seen, haven't felt. I'm richer for it."

He thought often about why he believed he wanted to teach English, about why English is the most-taught subject in American schools—the most-taught but sometimes the most-hated. He read the theories and found in each something good or bad or both. He read that at one time in the twentieth century a group of polled English teachers voted that their most important task was the eradication of slang, and he groaned, thinking of Shakespeare, whose slang became immortal.

And he read of other teachers to whom *ain't* was **THE ENEMY** and who devoted their lives to head-on assaults against it. Their brothers were the college teachers who automatically gave failing grades to any composition that contained a comma splice, a sentence fragment, or three misspelled words. Their cousins were the defiled defiling definers who insisted on rote memorization of the words of the book: "A simile is the statement of a comparison employing *like* or *as*," intentional fallacy is . . . , hovering accent is . . . , archetype means . . . , anacrusis is . . . And he knew that if such pettinesses were to rule his life he would lose his self-respect, would wither without flowering, would be paid society's money without contributing to society.

Some of his professors were brilliant men and women who felt literature and made their students feel. Others, often the most rewarded and honored by their universities, were noncontributors save to the scholarly journals and to their own satellites who were being groomed to become noncontributors save to the scholarly journals and to *their* satellites . . . He did not oppose research, even the trivia that filled many of the journal pages, but in his mind he insisted that if *he* ever did research, it must not be at the cost of his students, at the cost of himself as a human being,

at the cost of literature. Research should broaden a man, but too often it narrowed. He feared and hated not research but what research sometimes does to a man.

Still wondering why one teaches or studies English, he read the theories concerning organization of the curriculum. He saw the picture of the tripod, with legs labeled "composition," "language," and "literature," each leg the same length, with the unannounced implication that the whole thing would topple if someone sawed off a couple of inches or added a couple to one of the legs. He envisioned a photographer's or a surveyor's tripod, with a working mechanism at the top, the excuse for the tripod's being. But the English tripod was simply three legs that came together, with nothing at the apex. There was no working mechanism, nothing to give unity and purpose. The concept of the tripod might keep a teacher from forgetting an essential part of English, but it provided little help in the search for purpose.

The spiral was another visual device much loved by the curricular theorists. Any topic might be introduced on the first ring of the spiral (or any other) and reintroduced and amplified and strengthened on any other ring. The New Math spiraled its way upward, with basic algebra or trigonometry presented very early and gradually added to. He was a little bothered when the young checkout girl in the supermarket had to count on her fingers to subtract a nineteen-cent overcharge but charitably decided that she was an atypical product of the New Math. And he wondered to what extent English lent itself to an organization that might be highly suitable for mathematics or biology, since English, one of the humanities, was far from neatly categorized. Did English conform to a neat taxonomy? A red-tailed hawk belongs to the Animal Kingdom, the phylum Chordata, the subphylum Vertebrata, the order Falconiformes, the family Accipitridae, the genus Buteo, and the species Borealis. But could and should one taxonomize similarly a sonnet, a semicolon, a metaphor, a composition written by Susie Simpson? To what avail? And is there indeed a sequence ("cumulative sequence," the curriculum builders liked to say) in this subject called English? If so, can subject-sequence be divorced from child-sequence, the varying growth-rates of this child and that?

He read about the theory that English is equivalent to Communication. Communication is divided into two parts: Sending and Receiving. Sending is subdivided into two parts: Speaking and Writing. Receiving is subdivided into two parts also: Listening and Reading. He liked this theory a little better. Communication is something the child does. This theory did not mainly anatomize the subject; it considered the child especially. Yet still he felt uneasy, because the English=Communication theory was not new, had been around for decades, but had effected no great improvements. Perhaps the trouble lay in what went on under the four subheadings. If writing, for example, was

badly taught, the validity of the theory itself was not suspect.

He read that English is a unified subject and that this fact should govern curricular planning. But Expert A said that *language* provides the unity, and Expert B insisted that *literature* provides it, and the weak little voice of Expert C said that *composition* is the unifying force. Expert A prepared a curriculum that was very strong in language and paid too little heed to literature and composition. And Expert B prepared a curriculum that . . .

In his search for purpose, he read whole issues of the *English Journal* and found many purposes stated or implied. Many of the authors, most of the authors, he supposed, were excellent teachers. They followed no single formula. Their procedures were different; their values were different; their aims, though often akin, were obviously not identical. Maybe, he thought, there is no royal road, no highway, no clear destination, maybe only an infinite number of paths and byways, each with its own pleasant scenery, its own hills and creeks and waterfalls, with no mountaintop ever seen or to be sought.

He read the Dixon and Muller reports on the Dartmouth Seminar, which was a 1966 assemblage of a group of teachers and professors from England, Canada, and the United States. As he read *Growth through English*[1] and *The Uses of English*,[2] he became excited

[1] John Dixon, (Reading, England: National Association for the Teaching of English, 1967).
[2] Herbert J. Muller, (New York: Holt, Rinehart and Winston, Inc., 1967).

about what was happening in British schools. Child involvement was the theme. British children were not reading about literature. In a sense they were not reading literature; rather they were living *in* literature, taking part in pantomimes and dramatizations of literature, imagining how they would have reacted had they been in the place of a character, arguing about literature, imitating in their own writing if not literature at least the spirit of literature. And in their writing they did not compose "themes," neat and vague or precise fulfilling of assignments. They wrote their hearts, their growing minds, their emotions, their grasping fluttering surging groping. They did not study language—they were dreadfully ignorant of language, he thought—but they used language constantly. They didn't know that language has a history, but sometimes with language they could catch in a phrase the errant flight of a butterfly or the tingle that came with holding a small winning ticket in a lottery.

As a sophomore or junior, after he had definitely decided that he wanted to teach English, he tried to pull pieces together, still searching for purpose. What he came out with, he knew, might satisfy no one except himself, and might change for him. For each person, in the end, cannot accept another's goal. If there were complete conformity, there would be sterility and lockstep, a dying of imagination, a failure to catch the golden moment, the impossibility of innovation or fresh insight or adventure or following a trickle to discover its

source or the stream into which it flows.

What he came out with he put down in his scrawling hand. It read like this:

1. English is not important. A language is a learned, unique but constantly changing vocal system, composed of arbitrary symbols, used for communication within a culture. As such, it is a mere physical thing, an endless melange of sound waves or their artificial transformation into ink on paper. In itself the English language, or any other, has no more surface significance than the physical aggregation of atoms and molecules in a boulder or a peach tree, or the concatenation of sounds in a storm at sea.

2. But what is done with English, or any other language, is important. Some three billion human beings populate the globe, over two hundred million in the United States alone. Crowded on their tiny planet (six-sevenths water), pushed increasingly into elbow-to-elbow metropolises, dwellers in man-made cliffs of brick and concrete and glass, they bump unceasingly into their fellows, work with them in offices and factories, go to concerts and ball games by the thousands, play in the streets, drink in the saloons, make love and bring up children, and search. Search, if not for the meaning of life, at least for the meaning *for me.* All these things need words, and the wiser the words the wiser the life. Words may reflect anger, hostility, fear, hatred, and benevolence, humility, patience, love. Language may soothe the tired moment, reduce frustration, give a child insight, get a

job done. It contributes to the search.

3. What I must do in my teaching is to bring child and language together. Language in its many forms. The child with his many needs. The child as a receiver and a user of language. The sweet-talk of the politician and the TV commercial, which all his life the child will have to judge. The literature that can speak to the child, open gates, show ideals, help him to feel the ramified emotions that have impelled man since Adam. Language as a tool and more-than-tool—language for labor and language for play and language for revelation. The way language works, the way the English language works. Using language to present and to conceal. Using language to understand self and to clarify for others. Never language alone, but always language in relation to the child.

4. I conceive of the value of English as three-fold, so my work must be three-fold. On the lowest level is the mechanical, the manipulative (sometimes but not always imposed by society) artificial constraints: use a comma here but not there, spell *benefited* with one *t*, write legibly, learn to read faster and with more understanding. On the second level is the informative: how coherence is attained, how words affect people, how an author works, how literature differs from science, what the functions of metaphor are, how lyric differs from narrative, what insights into humanity are revealed in this story, truths about people. On the third level is the esthetic: the sources of beauty, the relationship of literature to human-ity and the humanities, the language of art and the art of language. I must juggle, keeping three balls in the air at once. Society prizes the mechanical, and it can indeed be worth mastering if the teacher doesn't consider it the grand prize. But I must never let a child, no matter how dull, think I have no more to offer him. He must see the other two balls simultaneously in the air. The information is of a kind he cannot find in an encyclopedia or in his science book. And in my class he must glimpse beauty daily, for daily beauty makes search for beauty habitual.

Such were his mused scrawlings when he had decided for certain that the teaching of English should be his life's work.

He looked with eyes more open on his college courses. What did they offer him? What did they lack? What would he have to learn on his own?

He looked more critically at his professors, tried to guess their motivations, analyzed their successes, wondered at their occasional or frequent failures. No two professors were alike, except that almost all but the best wore a halo of certainty, for they were Authorities on their subject: "I am Sir Oracle, And when I ope my lips, let no dogs bark." The best had no haloes and did not hesitate to say "I don't know" or "I'm not sure. Let's try to find out." Those professors he trusted, and he tried to enrol again in their courses.

He started making a list of what he would still like to learn while in college, and as he learned more, the list grew, because he knew more things to ask questions about, and when he graduated, even though he had tentatively crossed off many questions, the list was very long indeed, and very haphazard. He groaned each time he saw its length and knew that never would he or anyone else be able to cross off all the questions. But college had helped him in his search, even though his list was longer than it had been two or three years previously. And he knew that throughout his life he would cross off questions (tentatively) and add more.

On graduation day, he thought to himself, "Commencement. An appropriate name, as the speaker will probably tell us. I'm just beginning. There's so much I don't know that I need to know. I've not read enough, not thought enough, not learned enough about young people. I'll have to keep on learning. I must never stop. The gaps in my knowledge—the gaps horrify me. I've tried to fill many of them, but unsuspected ones keep appearing.

"Am I alone in recognizing gaps? Probably not, judging from conversations with other seniors. Not just English teachers, either. Teachers of all sorts. And everybody else going into a profession. If I were going to be a bricklayer, maybe I wouldn't have so much still to learn. Bricks are less complicated than people."

He knew that he would have many experiences, inside and outside the classroom. He wondered why some people seem to learn so much more from experience than others do. Maybe it was because some people can do a better job of relating one thing to another. Like Professor Knight, who taught Victorian literature, but whose far-ranging mind kept relevantly bringing in atomic energy and turtles and Plato and supermarkets and his six-year-old daughter and the Spanish Armada and seemingly almost anything, and whatever he brought into the discussion seemed miraculously to cast light on Victorian literature. Tennyson's "Ulysses," the senior surmised, must be one of Professor Knight's favorites. How lovingly the professor had lingered on some of the lines:

> I will drink
> Life to the lees: all times I have enjoy'd
> Greatly, have suffer'd greatly, both with those
> That loved me, and alone; on shore, and when
> Thro' scudding drifts the rainy Hyades
> Vext the dim sea; I am become a name;
> For always roaming with a hungry heart
> Much have I seen and known: cities of men,
> And manners, climates, councils, governments,
> Myself not least, but honour'd of them all;
> And drunk delight of battle with my peers,
> Far on the ringing plains of windy Troy.
> I am a part of all that I have met.

"I too am a part of all that I have met," the graduating senior mused, "and all that I have met is part of me, and all that I'll ever meet will become part. It will all have some relationship to the job that I'll be doing, if I can only see the relationship. Let me look back often," he almost prayed, "let me look back often, but never to regret; let me look back only to learn."

1

Minimal	Good	Superior
An understanding of how language functions	A detailed knowledge of how language functions, including knowledge of the principles of semantics	Sufficient knowledge to illustrate richly and specifically the areas listed under "good"
A reasonably detailed knowledge of one system of English grammar and a working familiarity with another system	A detailed knowledge of at least two systems of English grammar	
A knowledge of the present standards of educated usage; knowledge of the levels of usage and how those levels are determined	A thorough knowledge of levels of usage; some knowledge of social and geographical dialects; a realization of the cultural implications of both usage and dialect	
	A knowledge of the history of the English language, with appropriate awareness of its phonological, morphological and syntactic changes	

Knowledge of Language

Each chapter in this book will begin with an outline like the one to the left, adapted from ISCPET's "Qualifications of Secondary School Teachers of English: A Preliminary Statement," *College English*, 27 (November 1965), 166-169. The remainder of each chapter is intended to develop most of the points presented in the outline.

Some Misconceptions

Several misconceptions have hampered the teaching of the English language in the schools. Perhaps the worst of these is that "correctness" should be the chief aim of such instruction. Results: millions (billions? trillions?) of child-hours spent writing *was* or *were* in blanks; a feeling of inferiority in millions of persons because they have been made to believe that their English is not good; a contrasting snobbishness in many others because they are convinced that they are among the elite who use good English; a belief that "right" and "wrong" are absolute terms in language, as they may be in mathematics; [1] a hatred of English on the part of those who have difficulty in making their language conform to the teacher's expectations.

Another of the misconceptions is that knowledge of grammar leads inevitably to "correctness." So students have parsed and labeled and diagramed, and wept or sworn, according to their temperaments. Identifying was confused with using; the ability to recognize subjects was mistakenly supposed to assure the use of *he* rather than *him*.

A third misconception is that language study consists and should consist mainly or solely of grammar and usage. So what can be one of the liveliest, most exciting parts of the English curriculum has tended to be the dullest.

A fourth misconception is largely responsible for the first three. This is the voiced or unvoiced belief of many college English professors that only literature matters, that language study, except maybe for philology, is grubby and not a fitting

---

[1] However, awareness of relativity has decreased assurance of rightness and wrongness even in mathematics. According to Einstein, parallel lines may meet somewhere in infinity, and, in some mathematical systems, 2 plus 2 is not necessarily 4.

activity for the best minds; or else that language is so simple that no one need study it on the college level. As a result, most high school English teachers—prepared by the colleges—have engaged in no formal collegiate study of language or have taken no more than one course. Whole areas of language history, dialectology, and semantics and other branches of lexicology have remained unopened for these teachers, and in consequence they cannot open them for their students.

How Language Functions

Man's use of language is one of his greatest accomplishments and is responsible for civilization itself. Language distinguishes man from the lower animals, which, though some of them can communicate after a fashion, merely repeat the same sounds over and over: no lower animal constructs a sentence. Because man has sentences, he can link concepts and say things that no other man has said; such linking is the basis of thought processes. Because man has sentences, he can progress from where he is to somewhere else. He can conceive of and build the Taj Mahal or a submarine or a spaceship; he can find a preventive for smallpox or a cure for tuberculosis; he can write the *Divine Comedy* or *Giants in the Earth.*

No one knows exactly how to explain the miracle of language, though linguists and psycholinguists and sociolinguists and others are building little by little our understanding. Linguistic competence, we are now told, is an innate human characteristic, but linguistic performance must be learned. That is, the capacity to apply names, to construct sentences, and to join sentences coherently is inborn, but if a child grew up in an environment in which no one ever communicated with him, he would never learn to develop in performance, to communicate in other than animalistic ways.

Experience must come first. To talk about cows, one must have experience of some kind with cows—seeing them, seeing pictures of them, distinguishing them from horses or dogs. A concept of cowness must develop. The richer the experience, the clearer the concept.

Then comes the application of the name to the experience. The small child, after enough acquaintance with cows, and after hearing older people say "cow" to designate a particular creature, himself says "cow" when he sees one or a picture of one. He may make a mistake, of course, and call a sheep a cow, but

4

gradually he differentiates until unerringly he can say "cow" when the proper stimulus arises.

The isolated word, based on experience, comes early (though inevitably preceded by crying, cooing, babbling, jabbering, learning the operations of the human noise-making apparatus). If the child's language stopped with the word or with a dozen or a few dozen words, he would not surpass in language a crow or a dolphin, each of which utters sounds akin to isolated human words.

On a great day in the life of the child, he echoes a word-combination he has heard and speaks his first sentence; his mother excitedly writes it in his Baby Book. On the greatest day in the life of the child, he constructs a sentence he has never heard before, and the door of true communication is pushed ajar. From here he can move as far as his mental ability, his experiences, and his ambition can take him. Even though his first "original" sentence is no more than "Daddy come" or "Cow say moo," he has accomplished the tremendous feat of associating his experiences of cows with the word *cow*, his experiences of saying with the word *say*, and his experiences of mooing with the word *moo*. He has linked together the three words, representing these experiences, in a pattern learned through imitation. "Cow say moo" reflects a mind at work; it involves countless neural connections that no psychologist can yet define precisely.

The niceties and the elaborations come later: learning when to say *the* before *cow* and other words; distinguishing *say* and *says* and *said*; differentiating singular from plural; adding modifiers; building generalizations . . . the list can be indefinitely long. The learning proceeds at different rates with different children. The neural connections, like the wiring in an infinitely complex computer, may be less satisfactory in some children than in others, and the experiences in the home, in the street, and at school are not the same for all. For reasons beyond their control, some fourteen-year-olds even on the playground seldom construct a sentence they have never heard before; they talk and shout repetitiously. Other fourteen-year-olds are remarkably articulate, combining words (and the concepts that the words represent) in endlessly unique ways. And both kinds of fourteen-year-olds, along with even more in-betweens, are in the English teacher's classes.

What should be done with them? Better, what should be

done with each? Each is at one stage of development, and more advanced stages lie ahead of each. The stages cannot be overleaped or bypassed. Each must move through them one by one. The child with the poor neural connections or the deprived environment will move more slowly. The gap constantly widens between him and the others. But the steps toward growth are the same for all: adding to experiences, learning the words that designate the experiences, connecting the experiences. The classroom is an experience-adder, a broadener, a place where one talks about experiences, learns the words, makes connections. It is not a place for abstract theorizing about language (until the stage of abstract theorizing has been reached), but it is a place for using language, playing with language, examining concepts, relating today's concepts to yesterday's.

The linguists have much to say about the workings of language, much that can be used in the classroom. Harold Allen summarizes eight axioms:

1. Language is system.
2. Language is vocal.
3. Language is composed of arbitrary symbols.
4. Language is unique.
5. Language is made up of habits.
6. Language is for communication.
7. Language relates to the culture in which it occurs.
8. Language changes.[2]

A college course (preferably courses) in linguistics is necessary for a teacher to understand the implications of all eight points. In part of his discussion of the first point, for example, Allen says:

> . . . recognizing the complexity of the system we see how the English sentence is composed of layer upon layer, not of a series of units in a row as viewed in old-fashioned parsing. We see how in spaces or slots within these structures we can put either single or other complex structures, and for the first time we find an ordered approach to the problem of helping our students develop maturity in writing English prose. We can now plan a sequence of structural content through all the grades, without the painful and repetitive review that has justifiably alienated so many students.[3]

We cannot here describe a system such as Allen has in mind, because a whole book would be needed. Such books, constantly

---

[2] "A Pharos for the Institute," in *The English Language in the School Program,* ed. Robert F. Hogan (Champaign, Ill.: National Council of Teachers of English, 1966), p. 3.

[3] *Ibid.,* p. 4.

6

updated as linguists discover more truths about language, exist and are used in good college courses. The minutiae are not important, nor the disagreements among linguists about a particular classification, but an understanding of the layers of language, the system of the language, is essential for any teacher who wants to develop his students' comprehension of the workings of English.

The sixth of Allen's axioms, that language is for communication, deserves special attention. The statement is mainly true, even though one can argue that a second purpose of language is to clarify one's own feelings and thoughts and beliefs rather than to communicate them to others. Most of the time we use language to convey some sort of message to someone else. Business and industry, in fact almost all the components of civilization, depend upon language. The first impression and the lasting impressions that one makes upon others are also largely attributable to what one says and how he says it. Language reveals the self—ideas, attitudes, interests, thought habits, personality, character.

The words one chooses reveal oneself and influence others. Here semantics enters in. One of the definitions of semantics in Webster III is this:

> the study dealing with the relations between signs and what they refer to, the relations between the signs of a system, and human behavior in reaction to signs including unconscious attitudes, influences of social institutions, and epistemological and linguistic assumptions.

The "signs" here are, of course, symbols, especially words as symbols. Semanticists are insistent upon the symbolic nature of language. The word is not the thing; the map is not the country. The symbols, though, affect human behavior: people may be swayed by words as Alexander was swayed by the music of Timotheus. The symbols favored by a society reflect the society: "God save the King!" "Heil Hitler!" "Stand up for democracy!" "Down with American imperialism!"

As one who deals constantly with words, an English teacher should know at least basic semantics, but many college preparatory programs provide little or no instruction in it.

Grammars

Studies made in the 1940's and early 1950's suggest that at that time about half of high school English class hours were

7

devoted to grammar and usage, but the Squire-Applebee study reported in 1968 that the time allotted to language study had dwindled to 13.5 percent.[4] Among the reasons for the decline are decreasing faith in the efficacy of grammatical instruction and great teacher confusion about the new grammars that were being developed.

The grammar traditionally taught in the schools was Latin-based and prescriptive. Though it was less bad than intemperate critics have declared, it was filled with inconsistencies (for example, in its definitions of parts of speech), it tried to fit a Teutonic language into a Latin mold, and it said to students, "This is the way you should express yourself" rather than "This is the way the language is."

Structural grammar, in contrast, attempts to describe the language as it is. Using a corpus—almost always a corpus of *spoken* language—it analyzes methodically, with special attention to phonological patterns. It redefines the parts of speech, dividing them basically into form classes (which traditionalists would call nouns, verbs, adjectives, and adverbs) and function words (pronouns, prepositions, conjunctions, and a miscellaneous assortment including *the*, *very*, and other specific words).

Transformational-generative grammar is concerned not with description of a corpus but with the ways that sentences are produced. Although its proponents now contradict a number of things they themselves said earlier, basically they believe that children learn early a system for producing "kernel" sentences and then learn to effect transformations by means of which kernels are added to, made passive, changed to negatives or interrogatives, etc. Through "feature analysis" the transformationalists have recently been describing the deep structures underlying the surface structure of every sentence.

Other kinds of grammar, and variations of these three, have been proposed. Among them are the tagmemic system of Kenneth Pike of Michigan, the stratificational grammar of Sidney Lamb of Yale, and the sectoral grammar of Robert Allen of Columbia. So far none of these has been extensively taught in colleges and hence not in the schools.

We are obviously living, then, in a period of grammatical flux and uncertainty. A teacher is faced with choices like these:

1. Teach no grammar at all, on the ground that traditional

---

[4] James R. Squire and Roger K. Applebee, *High School English Instruction Today* (New York: Appleton-Century-Crofts, 1968), p. 140.

grammar didn't seem to help students much, so why should any other be expected to do so? 2. Again, teach no grammar at all, but this time on the ground that since scholars are not in agreement about the most accurate way to describe language, certainly a teacher cannot be sure to make the best choice. "Let's wait until scholars tell us what the truth is." 3. Teach traditional grammar, on the ground that it has long been taught and its terminology is fairly familiar to the adult public. 4. Teach one of the newer grammars, on the ground that traditional has proved inadequate and something different should be given a chance. 5. Select from various grammars whatever will clarify important principles for students.

To make a choice, the teacher must decide whether the teaching of grammar has any value and, if so, what the values are. Research reports on the usefulness of traditional grammar in the improvement of composition and usage have been generally negative. Those on structural and transformational have been mixed, but more positive than negative; in particular, as the report by Donald A. Bateman and Frank J. Zidonis indicates, a higher proportion of well-formed, mature sentences appears to result from practice with transformations.

Another possible value of grammatical study is cultural. Certainly students should have a chance to learn in reasonable detail about that which makes man man, his use of language. The study of grammar is in part the study of complex mental operations. It is the study of clarity vs. muddiness or ambiguity. It is the study of man's most precious tool. When a student realizes, by a study of deep structure, the complicated processes that his own mind goes through in constructing sentences, when he gains an awareness and appreciation of the marvelous sentence-machine that operates inside himself—operates even though he believes he is "slow"—he attains a greater respect for himself and for human beings in general.

The usefulness of grammar in the teaching of reading has been demonstrated by, among others, the late C. C. Fries and by Carl Lefevre and Ronald Wardhaugh. And scholars are beginning to awaken to the fact that grammatical knowledge can be useful in the study of literature. At the Dartmouth Seminar a linguist and a literary critic each had a go at explicating a difficult poem. The linguist admitted that the critic clarified parts of the poem that he could not, and the literary critic returned the compliment. If the walls between the professors of language and the professors of literature are not exactly tumbling down, at least they're cracking in a few places.

None of the schools of grammar have a monopoly on truth and other virtues. On their side the traditionalists have—well, tradition, of course; their terminology is the most familiar and they've had a lot of practice in describing sentences. Besides, the traditionalists have the force of public opinion; most administrators and parents were taught traditional grammar and don't trust newfangled stuff very much, mainly because English teachers haven't done enough to familiarize them with the strengths of more recent modes of analysis. The structuralists, with their emphasis on the spoken language, have much to offer on tone, pitch, and juncture. The transformationalists have developed a working model of the way we generate sentences, thus contributing new insights into syntax. The well-prepared teacher, though he may prefer one grammar to the others, should be able to draw upon more than one in his discussion of language with his students.

Usage and Dialectology

Grammar should be only one of the language concerns of the teacher. Usage is another. The two are often confused, with "grammar" being named when "usage" is meant. Grammar is the description of a language. Usage, to quote Webster III again, is "the way in which words and phrases are actually used (as in a particular form or sense) generally or among a community or group of persons: customary use of language." Thus, if one describes the subject-predicate structure of a sentence, he is dealing with grammar, but he is talking about usage if he observes that most educated speakers say "have gone" but a large number of other persons say "have went." Or, for other examples of usage, some persons distinguish between "continual" and "continuous," but others do not, and a few people say "I shall," but most say "I will."

Grammar is based on usage. The "well-formed" sentences that some transformationalists like to talk about involve descriptions of the structures and usages that happen to represent the language of the prestigious at a given time. Thus after the subject *they* the transformationalist's sentence tree shows a V_{pl} (plural verb) rather than a V_s (singular verb), showing that "they were" is grammatical but "they was" is not.

Dialect is related to usage, also. A dialect may be defined as a collection of usages (including not only words and phrases but also pronunciations) characteristic of a certain individual or group.

Usage is cometimes classified by levels from "formal" to "nonstandard," but the levels are so imprecise and shifty that some modern dictionaries have dispensed with them. In the eighteenth century, Swift would have labeled *mob* nonstandard or slang or "corrupt English"; a century later, British scholars considered *advocate, belittle* and *governmental* mere Americanisms; only three or four decades ago *reminisce* was nonstandard. Conversely, the double negative was long respectable, as was the double superlative (Shakespeare's "most unkindest cut"), and America's respected founding fathers regularly used *ain't* in their conversation and personal letters. Since usage does change, the terms "right" and "wrong" are hardly appropriate, though we can say with honesty and reasonable accuracy that a given expression, such as *I seen,* is "nonstandard" at a particular time.

The teacher should know in considerable detail the changing usages of English and should be able to acquaint his students with many of them. Change is gradual but constant in every living language, and today's "wrong" may be tomorrow's "right" or vice versa. Students feel less hemmed in if they know the realities of language instead of feeling that it is a straitjacket. Yet most of them want to be up to date and to conform to the usages of the present day, though without being slavish in their conformity. They themselves are often innovative in their language, and they should be encouraged to play with language, to experiment with it, to coin words and try out unusual sentence patterns.

The study of dialect, besides being informative in its own right, can enlarge understanding of usage. The study of American dialects is generally more meaningful to students than the study of Middle English dialects, though a teacher will find that knowing about British as well as American dialects can enrich his teaching. The contributions of linguistic geographers have been very helpful. They reveal, for instance, the areas in which people say *sick* (*to, at, in, with* or *from*) *one's stomach,* the areas that prefer *skillet* or *frying pan* or *fry pan* or *spider* or *creeper,* the varied pronunciations of *orange, news, roof, creek,* and *greasy,* the areas of preference for *dived* and *dove,* and infinitely more. Teachers report that dialect study often ranks near to the top in student appeal.

It has humane values, too. A Maryland teacher tells of a class that ridiculed one of their members who said, "My haid hurts." The teacher made no direct response, but read a story in which the characters spoke Pennsylvania German.

> When I questioned why Granny said, ". . . it makes time for supper," they again answered, "It was supper-time." Everyone agreed that the only difference was the way Granny spoke. To my question "Why did she speak differently?" came a reply: "Marguerite de Angeli is writing about a Pennsylvania Dutch family. That's the way they speak in that part of Pennsylvania." My next question, I hoped, would have a far-reaching effect into the incident with Carole. "If you were a part of the community in that area, would you speak the way Granny did or the way you are now speaking?" The answer, which I had been probing for, came. "Of course, we would speak like Granny. How else would we be able to understand the other people in our community?"
>
> . . . When people travel, they take the dialect of their area with them. This is the reason why some students pronounce a word differently from the way their teacher does. Furthermore, since no one regional dialect is superior to the others, we should not condemn dialectal differences as inferior speech or "bad" English.[5]

Besides geographical dialects, linguists talk of social dialects. In England, where class distinctions for centuries were more definite than they have ever been in the United States, the upper classes tended to speak in one way, the lower classes in a variety of other ways. Since the United States preaches the doctrine of equality, presumably we have no classes of society. Nevertheless, Americans do vary in such things as income, housing, level of education, types of employment, home environment, and speech. In earlier years, teachers attempted to make everybody's speech alike—to erase social as well as geographical dialects. The present tendency, however, is not to label "wrong" any dialectal variation but to discuss such variations and to indicate that some varieties through historical accident enjoy greater prestige than others. No student is told that his dialect is inferior, but he is afforded the opportunity to learn about other dialects and, if he chooses, to adopt as much of a prestige dialect as he wishes.

It helps to know that everyone speaks a dialect—a dialect imposed upon him unconsciously by his family, his friends, his

---

[5] Sister Walter Mara Mattheu, "A Linguistic Approach to a Social Problem," *Maryland English Journal,* 6 (Spring 1968), 15.

geographical region, the decades in which he was young, his travel or lack of travel, even his physiological and anatomical peculiarities. The dialect of an individual, which is as distinctive as fingerprints, is his idiolect. To attempt to make all the millions of idiolects conform to a mythical national norm is not only ridiculous but also impossible.

History of the Language

"All things are daily changing," Plutarch wrote. "I am not what once I was," said Horace, and Byron later echoed him. Spenser wrote the unfinished mutability cantos of *The Faerie Queene*, and Shelley said, "Nought may endure but mutability." Bryant advised

> Weep not that the world changes—did it keep
> A stable, changeless state, it were cause indeed to weep.

Language, a human creation, is constantly changing. Webster III in 1961 included 100,000 words that had not been in the 1934 edition, suggesting that every day in that twenty-seven-year span an average of ten new English words had been coined and gained enough acceptance to be registered in the dictionary. Besides those ten, countless others did not get in, including many highly technical terms of little general interest and also including large numbers of "nonce-words," created for a particular purpose on a single occasion and perhaps never again used. Children, as well as adults, coin such nonce-words. Robert Pooley, for example, tells of a little girl who said "Yippee!" when she learned that the family was going camping, but when she found that she would have to gather firewood and wash dishes, she said, "Unyippee!"

The girl was illustrating language play, linguistic experimentation, creation of a term to fill a need. During the exuberant Renaissance, such linguistic creativeness was almost a way of life. Shakespeare's audiences must have enjoyed his outrageous puns or he would have stopped making them. He coined words, too, or added meanings; in "the multitudinous seas incarnadine," for instance, he invented *multitudinous* and changed *incarnadine* from an adjective meaning pale red to a verb that ever since has had a bloody suggestiveness. Shakespeare's more learned predecessors and contemporaries concocted, usually on Greek or Latin bases, thousands of polysyllabic "inkhorn" terms that Shakespeare satirized in Holofernes in *Love's Labour's Lost*.

Growth in vocabulary, of course, has not been confined to the Renaissance and the modern period. On its Teutonic base the language has added tens of thousands of words from Latin, many thousands from ancient Greek and medieval and modern French, musical and other terms from Italian, sea terms and words for cooking from Dutch, other words from Portuguese, Spanish, Russian, Arabic, Oriental tongues, American Indian languages—in fact, from all over the world.

Language history is tied closely to the larger history of mankind. Had the Anglo-Saxons and their descendants remained untouched on their islands, had there been no Norman Conquest or Renaissance inflow or English seafarers or wars on the continent or a New World to explore and settle or a British Empire, the English language would be very different from what it is. But the British were in the mainstream of history, and their language reflects their struggles with the current.

Not only in vocabulary, though for young students that is the most dramatic manifestation. The language has changed remarkably during the past thousand years in pronunciation, morphology (word forms), and syntax. We say "I am" but Beowulf said "Ic eom," with *Ic* pronounced much like German *Ich*. Several English words shifted pronunciation dramatically: *green*, in its Middle English form *grene*, was pronounced something like *grainuh*; *ride* was about like *reeduh*; *bone* was similar in sound to *bawn*; and *mouse* was once about like *moose*.[6]

Alexander Pope rhymed *tea* with *obey* and *join* with *line*, suggesting that he and his contemporaries said *tay* and *jine*. Many of them also said *goold* for *gold* and *Lunnon* for *London*. In more recent times the pronunciation *genuWINE* has been largely abandoned, and *deef* for *deaf* has been generally overcome by *def*. Battles still go on in the pronunciation of such words as *coffee, tune, roof, greasy*, and many more.

Besides changes in vocabulary and pronunciation, and more basic to sentence structure, a significant loss of inflections has occurred. Sanskrit had eight cases for nouns, signified by inflectional endings; Latin had six, Old English five, but Modern

---

[6] We have assumed that many teachers and teachers-to-be are unfamiliar with phonetic or phonemic alphabets. Understanding of such alphabets, however, can make easier the comprehension of phonological discussions in textbooks for use in colleges and some high schools.

English has only two. In Old English, if one wanted to say "The fish swims" or "I see a fish," he would use *fisc*; for "of the fish," *fisces*; for "to the fish," *fisce*; the comparable plural forms were *fiscas*, *fisca* or *fiscana*, and *fiscum*. Modern English uses *fish* throughout except for the possessive *fish's* (plural *fishes'*). Verbs and adjectives likewise have lost inflectional endings. The greatest consequence has been that English has had to rely heavily on word order, whereas a language with many inflections can rely instead on the inflectional endings to convey meaning. Not only nouns have undergone this loss; verbs and adjectives have changed no less.

Syntactic patterns have also changed. We do not ask questions, for instance, as Elizabethans did. "Why stay we now?" and "Dismay'd not this our captains?" are representative Elizabethan questions, based on transformational rules that have now been supplanted. We do not handle negatives in quite the way that our ancestors did, long verb phrases (*might have been seeming to fall*) have developed, the passive voice has increased in frequency, sentences have become shorter in the past one hundred years, and many other major or minor syntactic changes have occurred. Knowledge of such changes can assist teachers and their students in reading earlier literature.

American English is not quite the same as British English, though H. L. Mencken was not completely justified in calling his three fat volumes *The American Language*. Students can be interested in the differences in vocabulary (*lorry* vs. *truck*, etc.), in pronunciation (*clahss* vs. *class*, etc.), and in spelling (*honour* vs. *honor*, etc.). They can be fascinated by the naming process that went on when colonists found unfamiliar animals and plants in the New World, and thus had to borrow words like *raccoon* or *persimmon* from the Indians or had to coin their own names such as *catbird* or *jack-in-the-pulpit*. The study of place names can also be absorbing; Indian names like *Wisconsin* (twenty-seven states have Indian names); descriptive names like *Flat Rock*; memorializing names like *Washington* or *McKeesport*; Biblical names like *Sharon* and *Mt. Eden*; humorous names like *Goodnight*, Texas, and *Truth or Consequences*, New Mexico; names reflecting American ideals like *Independence, Liberty-ville, New Athens*, or even *Rough-and-Ready*; and names derived from other languages like *Smackover*, Arkansas, from the French *Chemin Couvert*.

The point is that the teacher who has a detailed knowledge

of the history of the language in England and America can constantly enrich his teaching. He can show the language as it really is—vibrant, restless, changing as people change. He can teach literature more intelligently, too, if he knows the history of words and constructions.

Colleges have included too little English language instruction in their offerings for teachers. A course or courses in English grammars and a lively course in history of the English language are minimal. Wherever possible there should also be courses or parts of courses in semantics, in dialectology, and in lexicography (far too few teachers know how a dictionary is made and what it can and cannot do). Large colleges and universities should provide work in the philosophy of language, the sociology of language, and the psychology of language. Not all teachers-to-be can squeeze all these courses into a crowded curriculum, but they can get some of them as undergraduates and others when they return for summer school or inservice study.

America's children (and British children) have been cheated. Confined to sentence diagrams, workbook exercises, and recitations based on a textbook only, they have concluded that the study of language is dull and sterile, whereas it is really lively and fruitful. Young children enjoy language play, but we kill the potential Shakespeare by changing play to drudgery. If teachers are not excited about language, how can students be excited? If gold rust . . .

2

Minimal	Good	Superior
Ability to recognize such characteristics of good writing as substantial and relevant content; organization; clarity; appropriateness of tone; and accuracy in mechanics and usage	A well-developed ability to recognize such characteristics of good writing as substantial and relevant content; organization; clarity; appropriateness of tone; and accuracy in mechanics and usage	In addition to "good" competencies, a detailed knowledge of theories and history of rhetoric and of the development of English prose
A basic understanding of the processes of composing writings of various types	Perception of the complexities in the processes of composing writings of various types	Perception of the subtleties, as well as the complexities, in the processes of composing writings of various types
Ability to analyze and to communicate to students the specific strengths and weaknesses in their writing	Ability to analyze in detail the strengths and weaknesses in the writing of students and to communicate the analysis effectively	Ability to give highly perceptive analyses of the strengths and weaknesses in the writing of students, to communicate this exactly, and to motivate students toward greater and greater strengths
Ability to produce writing with at least a modicum of the characteristics noted above	Proficiency in producing writing with at least considerable strength in the characteristics noted above	Proficiency in producing writing of genuine power; ability and willingness to write for publication

Knowledge and Skill
in Written Composition
[Imaginative and
Expository]

Shakespeare on Composition

The trouble with an outline like the opposite is that it is an outline. People don't show through, or places, or things. No teacher shows through in "a modicum of characteristics." No child shows through in "substantial and relevant content." We need outlines and generalizing phrases, of course, to do the world's work, but God help education and God help the teacher and God help the child if there is inadequate translation to flesh and blood. A poem, written by a great hand, might do the job better than an outline.

> The poet's eye, in a fine frenzy rolling,
> Doth glance from heaven to earth, from earth to heaven,
> And as imagination bodies forth
> The form of things unknown, the poet's pen
> Turns them to shapes, and gives to airy nothing
> A local habitation and a name.

Shakespeare's half-dozen lines say more about composing than do many fat tomes. Think of "poet" not as verse-writer but in the old Greek sense of "maker, creator"—a maker of anything from a recipe or a "theme" to an opera or a cathedral.

The maker glances "from heaven to earth, from earth to heaven," an essential step in the composing process. What in the universe's multitude of possibilities belongs here? What do I believe about what I am making? What do the pieces add up to? In the whole realm of *may be*, what do I think this means? How do I feel about it? How do I want to make someone else feel?

"Imagination bodies forth/ The form of things unknown." I am a creator. That which was not will be. I shape things unknown. I change form to body. Through the mysterious chemistry of my brain I can make corporeal the intangible. If I were a

19

Dickinson, I could capture the essence of a train, of traindom, licking the valleys up and stepping around a pile of mountains and peering superciliously into shanties. If I were a Melville, I could incarnate brooding evil. But since I am not Melville or Dickinson, maybe I can make someone feel as I felt, alone on a stormy night with my sick little brother, when the electricity was off for two hours.

The maker "gives to airy nothing/ A local habitation and a name." Shakespeare was a master at doing what he prescribed. Viola, in *Twelfth Night*, describing her mythical sister (really herself) "pining in thought," did not say that her sister was patient but that "She sat like patience on a monument." What could be more patient than a monument to Patience? The abstract patience is thin, airy, incorporeal, but Patience on a monument stands firm and three-dimensional through sun and snow. Small children share Shakespeare's preference for the tangible, though probably only because they haven't yet learned much about abstracting, and so they define functionally, concretely: "A hole is to dig." "A hole is nothing with dirt around it." "Happiness is an ice cream cone with nuts on top of it." But reality fades to the dull and often untrue generality of the college freshman: "The automobile is a mechanism fascinating to everyone in all its diverse manifestations and in every conceivable kind of situation or circumstance." [1] The student who writes like that needs to be brought back to ice cream cones with nuts on top.

What Should Children Write About?

What should children write about? What they know and what they feel and what they imagine. The student who wrote about the "diverse manifestations" of the automobile wasn't really writing about what he knows and feels about automobiles. He was merely writing language, pompous inflated language; he was writing ink, not thought or emotion. Doubtless he knew automobiles, had taken long trips in them, had outraced the wind on superhighways, had parked with his girlfriend on a lonely byroad, perhaps had visited an assembly line, maybe in grease-stained happiness had dismantled and reassembled an engine. But his mistaken teachers had encouraged him to write

---

[1] Quoted in Ken Macrorie, *Writing to Be Read* (New York: Hayden Book Company, Inc., 1968), p. 6.

emptily on "diverse manifestations" instead! A diverse manifestation had brought him an A; an overhauled transmission a C. "Use ungreasy language, children. Clean it up. Don't tell it like it is—I mean 'as it is.' Think big thoughts, think manifestations and not spark plugs. Hide what you feel. Never say *I*. And never make a comma splice or they'll flunk you at the University. If you write about manifestations and don't commit crimes like comma splices, you can pass."

The teachers didn't quite say such horrible things, of course, but he inferred them. Once when he wrote from his heart about standing helpless while a child almost drowned, the comment was "Use more varied sentence structure." And when a junior girl, having read in the Brownings, submitted her own limping variant of "How Do I Love Thee?" in lieu of a critical analysis, the comment read, "Does not fit the assignment. F. Rewrite." Word gets around. And diverse manifestations become frequent.

Truth, not deception, should be the student's goal in writing and should be the teacher's goal in praising. If there is truth, there will inevitably be the "substantial and relevant content" that our outline-makers admire.

Truth isn't always pretty. David Holbrook's children, for example, many of whom are "the rejected," know a world in which some of the ingredients are drunkenness, gambling, drug addiction, prostitution.[2] Holbrook doesn't tell them to stay away from these things and to write about diverse manifestations. He encourages them to write truth as they see it. Little truths lead them slowly to bigger truths. Through reading and talking they find that larger worlds surround their little world. But they have to start where they are.

(Parenthesis: A Wisconsin nun said, "Let's not blame the parents for the children they send us. After all, they send us the best they have.")

Substantial and relevant content is not the same for every child or for every age. Truth is the essence: what is true for this child at his stage of maturity with regard to this subject. It has been said that an ideal progression exists in subject matter of compositions, from "I" to "They" to "That"; in other words from the self-centered to the other-person-centered to the impersonal and the abstract. There is some wisdom in that observation, for the opening of gates should lead the child to an

---

[2] *English for the Rejected* (Cambridge: Cambridge University Press, 1964).

awareness of what is outside himself, beyond his immediate sur-roundings—to the people in books and in country or city, to the farm or the ocean he has never seen, to ideas he did not grow up with. But the progression does not occur at the same rate in all children. And even when a child has moved to "They" and "That," the self must still enter, the child in relation to this beyond-child subject, the persona, the point of view. "I" must still be in "They" and in "That." If it is not, the result is emptiness, dishonesty, a fog of words, diverse manifestations.

In the first quarter or so of the twentieth century, American students' compositions tended to be rather theoretical treat-ments of "The Effect of Third Parties in American Elections" or "The Contrasting Philosophies of Wordsworth and Coleridge." Then came a wave of creative writing, especially poems and short stories; but when the creative writers got to college, the instructors protested because many of the students hadn't been taught to outline and develop a tight little composition on "The Menace of the Nazis," and because some of them seemed to think that poetic license permitted considerable deviation from punc-tuation rules that the instructors considered essential if not sacred. So, with a shove from the colleges, there was a turn from creative writing to almost total emphasis on exposition and, especially in recent years, on literary explication. Structurally, the resultant compositions are often neat and tight, but in dic-tion they are frequently imprecise, and in style and content they are generally dull. So there are mutterings and unrest. Many English departments are asking whether they have not over-stressed expository writing, whether at least some attention to creative writing may not sharpen diction through the creator's constant search for the emotionally right word, whether stu-dents' style has to be dull, whether looking at a subject from an odd angle may not often improve content.

The British, especially until a child is fifteen or so, stress personal writing, frequently of an imaginative type, often improvisational, free-flowing, unhampered by conventional re-straints. Though the products are often the predictable trips to Mars, they sometimes are delightful playlets, sensitive short stories, nearly exquisite poems. When these children are a little older and their writing assignments are largely expository, their compositions reveal a carryover of freedom, whimsy, and aware-ness of nuances too seldom observable in the constipated prose of those who have never written anything except exposition.

American students, by and large, enjoy creative writing; average students enjoy it almost as much as do superior ones. In an unpublished doctoral dissertation, Robert J. Lacampagne reports answers obtained from several hundred carefully selected "superior" and "average" high school seniors scattered throughout the nation.[3] One question was "Do you find that your best writing originates most often from (a) literary sources; (b) personal experiences; (c) current events; (d) personal imagination; (e) models or examples of other writing?" Here are the results:

		Superior Students	Average Students
a	(literary sources)	23.6%	15.9%
b	(personal experience)	36.6%	34.9%
c	(current events)	6.0%	7.3%
d	(personal imagination)	31.5%	33.5%
e	(models)	2.3%	8.4%

Then the same students were asked, "Which of the following do you enjoy most? (a) personal writing; (b) journalistic writing; (c) research papers; (d) imaginative or creative writing; (e) essay or theme." Again the results:

		Superior Students	Average Students
a	(personal writing)	16.4%	23.9%
b	(journalistic writing)	4.1%	3.3%
c	(research papers)	7.1%	14.1%
d	(creative writing)	52.2%	40.7%
e	(essay or theme)	20.2%	18.0%

The *d* answers in both groups are especially revealing. About a third of all these students believe that imaginative writing is what they do best, and for almost half of them it is their favorite variety of writing.

Yet we have tended to reserve for superior students the goodies of composing poems, short stories, and other imaginative pieces and have placed many of our average and below-average students on a Spartan diet of business-letter writing, filling out forms, and doing workbook exercises. Such discrimination, however well-intended, is flagrantly unfair. Though all students should have much practice in exposition, they should all be

---

[3] "A National Study of Selected Attitudes and Approaches to Writing of Twelfth Grade Students with Superior Writing Performance versus Those with Average Writing Performance" (Urbana: University of Illinois, 1968).

allowed also to sharpen mental scissors and cut some of their pieces of writing from personally selected whole cloth.

The forms or genres of writing should vary. At no time after school days are over will a person have to write a "theme." He or she may write business letters, personal letters, memos, reports, after-dinner speeches, notes to the milkman, recipes requested by friends, garden-club presentations, or conceivably an occasional poem, story, or playlet. The writing the child does in school should prepare the adult for such varied tasks, but not necessarily by *ad hoc* methods that force every Bette to write a recipe. The point is simply that through a variety of writing assignments the child can learn principles and techniques of writing that later can be applied to whatever writing he may need to do.

Keeping the Reader in Mind

The child can learn much about "organization, clarity, appropriateness of tone, and accuracy in mechanics and usage." The one thing that all four of these have in common is that each implies a reader. The organization followed by the writer helps the reader to grasp the writer's ideas. Clarity of presentation prevents the reader from misunderstanding. Appropriateness of tone, though it has other facets, means appropriateness to the expected reader. And accuracy in mechanics and usage represents a bow to convention, an awareness that readers may be distracted and repelled by gross failure to conform to widely accepted standards of punctuation, spelling, verb choices, and the like.

Perhaps the most important thing to teach about organization is that *some* sort of organization is necessary for the assistance of the reader. The alphabetical arrangement of words in a dictionary or of names in a telephone directory is one form of organization. If the lexicographer or Bell Telephone arranged the words and names haphazardly, the user of their books would have to waste hours finding the information he wants and would probably give up in frustration and disgust. The reader of a short story or a novel expects and depends on some sort of chronological arrangement (though he can understand and forgive the use of flashbacks and other artistic devices that depart from strict time order). The person who wants to learn how to build an outdoor fireplace hopes to be told methodically what materials and tools he needs and the steps to follow in the construction. So teacher and students must realize that for the sake of the reader every piece of writing requires some underlying principle of organization.

The composition textbooks describe the various generally recognized principles: arrangement by time, by space, by comparison and contrast, by induction, and so on. They describe also the means of development within a pattern: example, illustration, definition, and so on. We shall not try to discuss any of the possible patterns here, but the teacher should know what they are and when each is appropriate.

And then give the students leeway. Though the teacher may believe that only one pattern of organization will suit a given topic, some students may see others—more imaginative ones, perhaps. For example, in a class that had set itself the task of drafting a protest to the Student Council concerning some cafeteria regulations, most students did what the teacher expected: prepared a list of complaints and one by one developed the reasons for each, concluding with a request for reforms. But one student wrote a short story instead—a relevant short story that dramatized what was wrong. The class chose his unorthodoxly organized presentation for submisssion to the Council.

Though organization must be taught, teaching it has risks that the teacher must guard against. It can stifle imagination. It can result in a dull recital of "firstly" through "tenthly." It can lead children to put pigeons into pigeonholes at a time when the birds should still be sweeping gracefully through the air.

Education, unfortunately, in large measure consists of development of inhibitions, and organizing represents an inhibition, one of the many school-imposed pressures toward conformity, which in turn are but part of the society-imposed pressures. The revolt of the hippies, or the less dramatic revolt in every generation, is a rebellion against such pressures. The hippies have a point: There is danger in enforcement of peas-in-a-pod similarity, a danger of becoming mechanistic, a danger of losing human values, a danger of choking to death the human imagination responsible for all true progress. But there is a point on the other side, too: if everybody "does his own thing" without regard to human context, anarchy results, and then who works in the factory or office, grows the wheat, delivers the mail, and collects the garbage?

The teacher straddles the line between anarchy and imposition, between freedom and discipline, between wild imaginative flights and methodical presentation. He sees value in both and in a way must encourage both. So he teaches organization, its principles and its values, but never insists that only one pattern is possible for a given purpose. American society permits freedom within limits, permits freedom but for the welfare of all must require some discipline. That is essentially what the teacher does in teaching organization.

It can be added that knowledge of organization can actually lead to greater freedom, in that it expands for the student his range of choices. If he has always written the chronological, his horizon is broadened when he realizes that sometimes an inductive method may be most convincing, or when he sees that for a newspaper account a special formula better meets the needs of his readers.

Further, the act of organizing is a thought-sharpener. Countless professional writers have said that they don't really know what they think about a subject until they write about it. Writing forces them to organize their knowledge and opinions, to weigh this piece of evidence against that, to look at the almost random collection of parts and sort out the relevant from the irrelevant and the substantial from the immaterial.

Writing is admittedly hard work, but it has the fascination of a puzzle. Of all the knowledge and emotions in the world, which ones belong here? Of all the pieces in this one little box, which ones fit together? Which may I safely discard? Which may I honestly discard? As for the pieces I have left, in what order should I put them together so that someone else can comprehend as closely as possible the picture that I have in my mind and be influenced to react to that picture in about the way that I do?

Once the puzzle is solved, the organization makes a large contribution to clarity. Although individual sentences or words may still be unclear to a reader, he will be able to understand essentially what the writer is driving at.

The unclear statement may have no apparent meaning or may have two possible meanings that the reader must unwillingly or uncertainly choose between. Always, though, the writer must have had some sort of meaning in mind, even though it may have been too fuzzily defined. What the teacher needs constantly to do is to emphasize the reader, who doesn't know what the writer means unless the writer tells him.

Intentional ambiguity is a virtue in a poem or other artistic creation, since with a single image it may call to the reader's mind two or more connotations, each of which enriches and enlightens. (William Empson, in *Seven Types of Ambiguity*, offers a bookful of examples.)[4] But unintentional ambiguity is what the teacher most often finds and must combat. Such ambiguity is of two kinds, lexical and structural. In "She likes interesting boys," is *interesting* an adjective or a gerund? Does she like boys who are interesting, or does she like to interest boys? In "six French teachers," are the teachers French or do they just teach French?[5]

Though perhaps no two problems in lack of clarity are precisely the same, any of them can be attacked on the grounds of mental cruelty to the reader. When children in small groups read one another's productions, they should become habituated to ask, "What does this mean? I don't understand this. Do you mean _____ or _____?"

Appropriateness of tone is also helpful to the reader, though in a more subtle way. Tone should be appropriate to the subject and the occasion, to the writer, and to the reader. It would be inappropriate to write humorously about the assassination of a President, because the subject or the occasion is not funny, and even to make harmless little jokes about it would be in bad taste. And it would not be appropriate for a student who knows a little about geology to write as if he were an expert, to use a tone that, if suitable for anyone, would befit only a scholar in the subject. Nor would it be appropriate to use the same tone in addressing a small child and one's fellow students and members of the school board.

Tone, especially with reference to the pose assumed by the writer in a given piece, is sometimes equated with voice, a term popularized by Walker Gibson. Gibson is also the author of one of the best treatments on contemporary style, *Tough, Sweet and Stuffy*.[6] Each style, says Gibson, is chiefly tough, like the writing of Hemingway, or sweet, like a commercial for face cream, or stuffy, like much federal prose. Gibson describes a "style machine," or criteria for measuring style. The tough style, which he considers generally more desirable than either

---

[4](New York: New Directions Publishing Corporation, 1930).

[5] Norman Stageberg, "Some Structural Ambiguities," *College English*, 47 (November 1958), 479–486.

[6] (Bloomington: Indiana University Press, 1966).

of the others, uses over 70 percent monosyllables, fewer than 10 percent polysyllables, an occasional *I* or *we*, many sentence subjects referring to people, few passives, few adjectives, few adjuncts, and relatively few dependent clauses.

One reason why many students write as they do is that some of their teachers, unlike Gibson, prefer sweetness or stuffiness to toughness. They give A's to pretty but unrealistic and trite descriptions of wavy grass and nodding violets in a field where "silence reigned supreme" save for the "droning buzz of a solitary bumblebee." Or they give A's to the pretentious, stodgy analysis of a literary work, an analysis filled with passives and polysyllables and space-filling but largely meaningless clauses like "It may safely be assumed that . . ." They often do not reward proportionately the direct, honest statement that "tells it like it is."

The conventions of mechanics are also intended to help the reader. The teacher should know of the lack of punctuation in ancient Greek manuscripts and those of the Hebrews and other nationalities, and he should have looked carefully at reproductions of some of the almost punctuationless manuscripts of early English scribes. He should know the debt we owe to the Italian Aldus Manutius, who first developed a systematic method of punctuating for clarity, a system we still follow today, with minor changes. Punctuation is not a set of rules but a set of conventions which, when agreed to and understood by both writer and reader, ease the task of communication. In other words, it is a tool, unimportant in itself but important as a means of helping the transfer of information or emotion from one mind to another.

The same is true of spelling. There's nothing preordained or sacred in the spellings *capital* and *capitol*, but if writer and reader both know that the spelling with *o* refers only to the building, understanding is easier. Or if a writer writes *pshylogy*, the reader may wonder whether the subject is *psychology* or *physiology*.

As for the misspellings that are not actually confusing, the point to be made is simply that any misspellings may be a distraction to the reader and may tend to lower his opinion of the writer. If the reader notes *their* for *there*, for example, he pauses to think "Careless fellow!" or "Ignorant fellow!" and may lose sight of the point the writer is trying to make. The same comment applies to matters of usage. "That day proved disappointing to Martha and I" is perfectly clear, but the educated reader is distracted by the *I* and may conclude that anything written by such an ignoramus is not worth reading.

The teacher should be sure, though, that he himself really is familiar with modern English usage and that he does not taboo something that is now quite respectable, such as a justifiable split infinitive, or starting a sentence with *and*, or the terminal preposition in "What did they talk about?" A reasonably permissive book like Margaret Bryant's *Current American Usage* [7] or Bergen and Cornelia Evans' *A Dictionary of Contemporary American Usage* [8] should be on his desk and its basic principles in his mind.

Some teachers have given English a bad name, we must add, by overemphasizing mechanics and usage. They are responsible for the frequent remark by otherwise intelligent adults, "Oh, you're an English teacher. I'd better be careful what I say!" Mechanics and usage are not ends in themselves, but only means. The communication comes first, finding something worthwhile to say, something that one can believe in and swear by and be emotionally involved in. The nitpicking, the quibbles about mechanics and usage, should not be allowed to interfere with the act of communicating. Inhibitions must not be built too soon.

Horrible example: A bright third-grade boy enjoyed writing in school. He wrote well, and his teacher praised him and didn't complain because he sometimes forgot a question mark or misspelled a word. Often at home in the evening he would sit down and voluntarily write a poem or a little story which he shared with his parents and, the next day, with the teacher and perhaps the class. Then he went into the fourth grade, where the teacher had him correct every misused comma, every misspelled word, every flawed sentence. He stopped all voluntary writing, and what had been developing into a colorful, individualistic style became a procession of short, dull sentences.

The familiar story of the centipede is one that every English teacher should recite to himself once a week. A recitable version got Mrs. Edward Craster into Bartlett's:

---

[7] (New York: Funk & Wagnalls, 1962).

[8] (New York: Random House, Inc., 1959).

> The centipede was happy quite
> Until a toad in fun
> Said, "Pray, which leg goes after which?"
> That worked her mind to such a pitch,
> She lay distracted in a ditch,
> Considering how to run.

We sometimes make children think so much about details that they too lose the ability to move their pens.

The Process of Writing

Composition used to mean assigning and correcting. "For Friday write five hundred words on _____." And then the teacher spent the weekend covering blue ink with red.

Today "process" is the word. Teachers don't just assign; they help in the composing. Especially in exposition the class explores together, sharing their knowledge of a topic and their experiences with it, arguing about interpretations, talking about and finding sources of more information, discussing possible approaches, considering ways of presenting data and ideas. Then each student chooses the variation of the topic that appeals to him, that conforms to his beliefs and feelings. Mindfull, he writes from knowledge and not from ignorance. He knows that it is not his responsibility to present a consensus; he need not conform to what the group or the teacher thinks; he may be himself. But he has to support what he says and perhaps contravene that which contradicts. He writes a draft. Members of a group of three or four read to one another what they have written. They agree with this, attack that, sometimes say "I don't understand that" or "An example would help" or "Doesn't the third point really belong before the second?" or "I don't know what you're really driving at." The teacher drifts from group to group, listening, answering questions. The student rewrites and hands in the result for the teacher's ministrations.

The saving in red ink is considerable. Students write fewer compositions, but better. They write what they know and believe. Writing is less artificial, more purposeful, much more informed. The teacher's frustrations—and each student's—are fewer.

Admittedly, we do not yet know enough about the writing process, just as we do not know enough about how children learn their native language. Professional authors exhibit at least superficial variations in process. Some plan meticulously in advance, but others do not. Angus Wilson, the novelist, plans details so meticulously that he fills sheets and sheets of paper with charts, maps, and floor plans, but Carl Van Doren declares that the pattern "largely takes care of itself." Perhaps Truman Capote is most representative; he plans rather carefully, but when he comes to the actual writing, "infinite surprises happen."

"Infinite surprises happen." Planning, knowing what one wants to say, is important, but students need to be led to realize that in the writing, new examples or even new ideas are bound to leap out, and if they are good they should be included. The "surprises" sometimes turn out to be the most vital part of a piece of writing. E. M. Forster, in planning *A Passage to India*, knew that "something important" would happen in the Malabar Caves, but not until he reached that point in his novel, in a scene that turned out to be pivotal, did he know just what the "something important" would be.

How important to process is the making of an outline, then? The answer varies according to the writer. Some sort of outline—not necessarily the formal I-A-1-a variety—is obviously desirable. But the outline should usually be regarded as a rough drawing, not a blueprint showing every detail. It can prevent haphazard presentation, but it should be flexible enough to admit any of Capote's "infinite surprises."

A word about inspiration. Some students claim that they cannot write unless they are "inspired"; they like to sit idly until the Muse descends and guides the pen. The experience of professional writers suggests, though, that inspiration is an illusion. Most of them work regular hours, and each day's stint may begin painfully. But they write, and keep at it, sometimes destroying the false starts, and eventually the words start to flow freely. For some writers, well along in a story, the characters take charge and in effect write their own story. William Faulkner said that for him this usually occurred about page 275, and added, "I don't know what would happen if I finished the book on page 274." For most students, probably the best advice is that inspiration comes from keeping the pen moving across the paper.

Rhetoric

The superior teacher of English, our outline declares, possesses "a detailed knowledge of theories and history of rhetoric and of the development of English prose." Even the neophyte can profit from some such knowledge, of course. Though much that has been written about rhetoric is dry as dust, much is provocative and may provide hints to be passed on to students as they become ready for them.

Classical rhetoric is not dead, as any reader of Edward P. J. Corbett's *Classical Rhetoric for the Modern Student* [9] or Father Daniel Fogarty's *Roots for a New Rhetoric* [10] knows. Plato's *Phaedrus* has been a staple item in many NDEA institutes for teachers. Aristotle's *Rhetoric* discusses persuasive devices as widely used in the twentieth century A.D. as they were in the fourth century B.C. Cicero's *inventio* (the finding of suitable arguments), *dispositio* (arrangement of the parts), and *elocutio* (diction and style) are still basic. Quintilian's advice that style should be suitable to the occasion has never been superseded.

True, classical rhetoric had its shortcomings. It dealt exclusively with persuasive speaking. We know that speaking differs from writing, and that persuasion is not the only goal of rhetoric unless *persuade* is very broadly defined. Modern rhetoricians are interested in writing and not just in speaking, and in exposition and evocative writing as well as in persuasion. Nevertheless, a teacher can still glean wise advice from the ancients.

The medievalists and early moderns have less to offer. Many of them were determined classifiers who used jawbreaking terms (*anacoluthon, anadiplosis, anaphora, anastrophe, antiphrasis* . . .) to describe relatively simple operations with language.

> All a rhetorician's rules
> But teach him how to name his tools.

Rhetoric, along with grammar and logic, was part of the "trivium" designated in medieval universities as a requirement for all seekers of the baccalaureate, but all too often it degen-

---

[9] (New York: Oxford University Press, 1965).
[10] (New York: Russell & Russell, Publishers, 1968).

erated into mere nomenclature that could be attached to appropriate segments of Latin or Greek oratory or literature. The eighteenth-century rhetoricians such as Blair, Campbell, and Whately were somewhat more practical but added little to the lore of the ancients. As a result of centuries of slight constructive effort and because of excessive emphasis on form as distinct from content, the term *rhetoric* fell into disrepute, and any unmeaty statement was contemptuously dismissed as "mere rhetoric."

But the twentieth century is witnessing a rebirth that is significant to teachers. Rhetoric is once more a tool of creation, not just an empty exercise in classification. The contributors to the revival (e.g., Kenneth Burke, I. A. Richards, Wayne Booth, Francis Christensen, Monroe C. Beardsley, Richard Ohmann) have relatively wide interests and do not hesitate to cross lines to psychology, sociology, philosophy, linguistics, psycholinguistics, and of course literature as they attempt to discover what choices a writer or speaker has and what determines or should determine the choices he makes. And since writing or speaking involves incessant choices, obviously the more a teacher knows about the possibilities, the more he has at his disposal as he guides students.

The choices are in content, organization, sentence structure, diction, "voice," and adaptation to the reader or audience. Many rhetoricians, ancient and modern, say much about content, organization, and adaptation. Francis Christensen and Kellogg Hunt and Richard Ohmann have studied sentence structure especially, analyzing how modern writers put together the parts of their sentences to attain specific effects. Walker Gibson says much that is wise about "voice," the stance assumed by a writer as he addresses himself to a particular topic and readership. The Fowlers, among others, have said some sensible and often-quoted things about diction, though diction is necessarily a part of voice. Ken Macrorie constantly emphasizes the human being whom rhetorical principles may serve. The point in this incomplete enumeration is only to suggest that many good minds have devoted and are devoting themselves to the development and application of rhetorical principles that a teacher can use in strengthening the compositions of his students.

Reacting to the Opening Mind

The pile of "themes" comes in. If process has been stressed, if students were saturated in their subject before they started writing, if they had a chance to try out one or two drafts on their friends, the themes are likely to be much better than themes usually are.

In the most modern British schools, the teacher doesn't do much with the themes. In fact, they may simply repose in each student's notebook until such time as the teacher chooses to thumb through the pages and write an occasional "Good" or "I like this." Or the teacher may read some selected pieces aloud or ask students to read their own, as a sharing of experience. In any event, except for the "upper form" students (corresponding to American high school juniors and seniors), papers are not returned with multiple corrections. As a result, British students in these schools are not grade-conscious about their writing. They write to communicate and to find themselves.

To find themselves. Perhaps American schools have not devoted enough attention to this objective. Perhaps in our grading we have been so much concerned with *things* (commas, etc.) that we have forgotten *people*. Composition may be communicative or expressive—expressive of the self, mind-searching, soul-searching. Perhaps we have overstressed the communicative and neglected the expressive. The act of putting words on paper, of organizing thoughts and feelings, may be self-revelatory. And in self-search, in self-revelation, anything goes. No subject is banned, no style or lack of style inappropriate. Ideally, all students should do much writing for themselves, for no other eyes, as they seek their own answers to Who am I? Why am I here? Where can I go? What can I do? What does it mean to me that I am black? What worries me? What can I do about it? But, practically, most students need encouragement, even prodding, to do their self-seeking. They may write mistrust, melancholy, hatred, uncertainty, inadequacy, the puzzles of puberty. They may write about the car they stole, the sexual experimentation, the lost boyfriend. Can such soul cries be graded? But aren't they important? Isn't the best comment often only "This moved me" or "Maybe you'd like to read _____"?

The communicative compositions can be marked. Always is heard an encouraging word. The teacher adjusts comments to the students. He diagnoses. What does this student need most? need first? Comments other than backpats are based on diagnosis. There is no point in telling a student that he needs everything. In general, comments should focus first on improvement of content, then on improvement in organization, later on mechanical flaws. But thirty different students may be at thirty slightly different stages. Writing comments is a fearsome business—to know who needs only the pat on the back, who is ready for some hard independent work on sentence structure, who must be helped to think a subject through, who . . . A fearsome business, playing at least a small-letter god with a developing mind.

The Teacher as Writer

Can a golf coach who never swings a club be successful? Can a shop foreman who never operates a machine do a good job? Can a writing teacher who never writes teach writing well? Probably not.

Not that the writing teacher has to be a professional. Few Thackerays or James Baldwins or James Restons are in classrooms (though an amazing number of British teachers and a fair number of American teachers are authors of published novels or short stories or articles or poems).

Not professional, but at least adequate. The teacher should be able to make ideas hang together in prose, should know how to make each sentence express a clear idea clearly, should have a precise knowledge of mechanics.

He should write frequently. If nothing more, he should write most assignments that his students are expected to fulfill. If they are to write a description, he should write a description. If they are to explicate a poem, he should explicate a poem. Sometimes his own compositions should be read or reproduced along with those of his students. One who has experienced birth pangs can best understand birth pangs. One who has experienced candid, constructive criticism can often become a more constructive critic.

Conclusion

Composing is a human activity. It is difficult, more so for some than for others. It enables human beings to reveal themselves, to themselves and to others. Its range extends from filling in an order blank to writing the *Iliad*. It is a tool and infinitely more than a tool. It reflects man working, seeking, thinking, feeling, living. It cannot be taught, but it must be learned, and learning can be guided.

College departments of English are beginning to provide more help than they once did. Formerly their composition offerings tended to be limited to freshman writing and perhaps a course in creative writing. Now many of them also offer advanced exposition, rhetorical theory and practice, composition for teachers, narrative writing, journalistic writing, and an array of courses in creative writing. Though obviously only a limited number of these can be wedged into a teacher-preparatory program, the colleges are at last making it possible to fill a serious gap in the preparation of many preservice and inservice teachers.

3

Minimal	Good	Superior
	An awareness that all literature is a reflection of the human condition	
Acquaintance with the most important works of major English and American authors	Familiarity with the important works of major English and American authors; knowledge of the characteristics of various genres and of major works in English literature in the genres	In addition to the "good" competencies: Intensive and extensive knowledge of one or more major authors and of at least one genre and one period; knowledge of major works of selected foreign writers, both ancient and modern, and of comparative literature
Awareness of the patterns of development of English and American literature from their beginnings to the present	As part of the awareness of patterns of development, a knowledge of such backgrounds of English and American literature as history, the Bible, mythology, and folklore	
Ability to read closely an unfamiliar text of average difficulty with comprehension of its content and salient literary characteristics	Ability to read closely an unfamiliar text of above-average difficulty with good comprehension of its content and literary characteristics	Familiarity with, and ability to make pertinent applications of, major critical theories and schools of criticism
	Familiarity with a considerable body of literature suitable for adolescents of varying abilities and backgrounds	

Knowledge and Skill in Literature

Why Teach Literature?

Why do we teach literature? Why do we want our students to read, read, read literature? Why do we hope that the reading of good books and good magazines will become a lifetime habit?

We can't prove that anyone gets a larger paycheck because he has read Chaucer or Swift or Thackeray or Melville. Nor can we prove that readers of Donne, Wordsworth, Dickinson, or even John Bunyan are morally better than persons who have never heard the names; we all know some near-illiterates whose adherence to conventional morality is much greater than that of some English majors. The justification for reading literature must be on grounds other than economics and morals.

Underlying any other justification must be that of pleasure. If one can read well, it's fun to read. If the reading of literature is not pleasant, almost no one will read voluntarily. If John Johnson while working with wood keeps scratching and cutting and hitting his fingers, he is likely to abandon his attempts, and if while reading he keeps being frustrated or bored or defeated, he is likely to do little reading. In an age that provides countless possibilities for pleasure, literature will be given a fair share of leisure time only if people like to read. If McLuhan is to be proved a false prophet—a very iffy *if*— literature has to demonstrate that it can provide satisfactions not obtainable from electronic gear, although films and TV programs can often supplement and add depth to the printed page.

Part of the satisfaction comes from the knowledge, the information, available through literature. This knowledge is not the same as that on the reference shelf; literature is not factual as an encyclopedia article is factual. As Matthew Arnold said, literature affords "a criticism of life," that is, a subjective peering into the recesses of life not penetrable by the tools of the physician or the psychologist. It shows what it means to be a human being—the joy and the anguish, the spirit and not just the body. Unlike the usual television fare that merely strings incidents together and concentrates on what happens, on the superficial trappings of life, literature is concerned with why things happen, on the motivations of man. Rather, the motivations of *a* man, for literature selects: it does not generalize or tabulate, but dramatizes the inner life of a man or a woman and lets the reader generalize if he will or apply to himself what is applicable.

Because it dramatizes in words of power, and because the literary artist is concerned with form and not just with content, literature offers an esthetic experience. At least it does if the reader reads well; if he does not, an esthetic experience becomes anesthetic experience. The old, old problem of the teacher of literature has been how to develop esthetic understanding without resorting to the tactics of the dissecter of a cadaver, how to show beauty without gushing about beauty, how to reveal the blend of art and substance that is the mark of every great writer.

Part of the pleasure may come too from an increased awareness of roots. Literature dramatizes the American heritage, the British heritage—the human heritage. Through it a reader can learn what it meant to be a pioneer wife, a soldier at Gettysburg, a poor boy in nineteenth-century England, a country squire, a Henry IV or V or VI, a medieval woman from Bath, a knight in a mead hall, a philosopher in ancient Greece. He can learn about his ancestors, how they lived, loved, thought. He can learn the continuity of the human experience. Rootlessness—or the unawareness of roots—is evil. It leads to excessive restlessness and dissatisfaction, even to anarchy, for if one thinks that he swims alone in the river of time, he will be lonely and uncertain. There is comfort, though, in knowing what others have undergone, in knowing that no one really swims alone and that one's ancestors have battled the same kinds of waves and currents and lived out their lives as the river of time flowed toward today and tomorrow.

From These Multitudes

The presses whir and roar. Twenty thousand, thirty thousand new books emerge from American binderies every year, and thousands of others in England, and uncounted more from other countries. Only a small portion, perhaps, have literary pretensions, but even that small portion may represent hundreds of books. The teacher cannot possibly read more than a fraction of a fraction of what might be teachable in an English class.

So to some extent he must be bound by tradition—though not completely. *Silas Marner* isn't the only novel suitable for sophomores, and Shakespeare did write some plays besides *A Midsummer Night's Dream* and *Julius Caesar* and *Macbeth*. It isn't necessary, then, to teach only what has customarily been taught, but one can nevertheless accept most of the judgments of the past concerning which authors and which works have deserved to survive. Poe or Whitman had hundreds of literary contemporaries, but in the winnowings of time most of the others have blown into doubtlessly deserved oblivion. There is seldom a reason for teaching the fifth-rate nineteenth-century author or even the second-rate.

The teacher needs to know the good from which he may choose. He will never teach all that he knows, and college professors of English even in teachers' colleges are justified in not concentrating just on those works most likely to be taught in high schools. A teacher should know more than he expects to teach, because he needs resources from which he can draw when the unexpected occasion arises, and he will be most comfortable when he has a large literary backlog.

So Beowulf and Virginia Woolf and Thomas Wolfe and perhaps even our contemporary Tom Wolfe should be in his ken. The shadowy Anglo-Saxon poets. Chaucer and his major contemporaries. The giants of the Renaissance. Some Donne and Milton and the Cavalier Poets certainly, and a glimpse of the Restoration dramatists. Swift, Pope, Addison, Steele, Gray, Johnson, Blake. The great Romantic writers and their Victorian descendants. Shaw, Joyce, Yeats, and the Angry Young Men who too soon stopped being angry or young. A little of the prosy prose of America's youthful days. Much of Emerson, Poe, and Thoreau, and bits of the now less idolized Longfellow, Whittier, Holmes. Heavily in Whitman and Melville and Mark Twain, and a dip into James and Howells. Dickinson, Frost, Cummings, and Eliot; O'Neill, Miller, and Williams; and Dreiser, Faulkner, Hemingway, Steinbeck, and other fictionists. An awareness of who is writing what today. This list is not exhaustive; a few score of other names could be justified. The teacher must be saturated in literature, versatile in his ability to glean from varied authors and ages the insights they provide into what a human being is and may hope to become. And since the dissemination of truth is not confined to prose or to poetry, the would-be teacher reads in all the genres and the subgenres, learning to interpret a delicate lyric or a strident ballad, learning to visualize from printed words the action on a stage, learning how short stories and novels may be constructed, learning of the vagaries of the essay from Bacon through Addison and Lamb and Emerson to its modern incarnation in the magazine article.

Though few high school teachers can truly be specialists, there are advantages in knowing one genre especially well. There is comfort in expertise, in being confident that there is one thing one knows or can do better than most of his colleagues. In team teaching, in departmental meetings, in curriculum planning, and in assisting beginning teachers, if a teacher has a recognized specialty he can make special contributions. So if somewhere in undergraduate preparation or in graduate courses he can learn in depth about drama, poetry, fiction, or the essay (or even about Greek drama, Renaissance drama, modern drama, the Theater of the Absurd), he may add to his value in the school and add his particular luster to the varied lusters of his colleagues.

The same sort of merit exists in knowing, more deeply than most, one or two major authors or one literary period. One Illinois high school teacher knows Shakespeare about as thoroughly as that complex author can be known, has read all his works several times, and is familiar with major Shakespearean criticism. Shakespeare is constantly useful to her, not just because of the quotable quotes that fit so many occasions, or because she is the "Shakespeare expert" in her department, but more important because her depth of knowledge of one author has given her literary insights into all authors: she can read almost any author intelligently and feelingly because she can read Shakespeare so well. Detailed knowledge of a literary period is helpful, too, especially because such knowledge helps to clarify how literature reflects an age but also to some extent transcends an age. One who knows well Dr. Johnson and his circle, for instance, can comprehend social and political and economic forces of the age, and when he leaves the Johnsonians and looks at the contemporary Gray,

Collins, the Whartons, and others, he sees foreshadowings of the literary developments of the Romantic Age.

Some awareness of the patterns of development of English and American literature is desirable, too. As literature in English marched through the centuries, it changed noticeably in content, language, style. Fads like those exhibited by the Euphuists or the metaphysical poets came and went and sometimes reappeared. Drama developed from the relatively simple morality or mystery to the complexity of Shakespeare and the very different complexity of Shaw. New genres of prose developed and flowered in the novel and the short story. There was a rebirth of classical learning, a neoclassical period, a romantic revolt, a turn toward realism and naturalism, and an eclectic period with much experimentation. The precise dates of such developments have only minor significance, but knowledge of the trends and their relationships to world events and to the nonliterary arts makes richer the teacher's grasp of literature.

Backgrounds

Literature does not exist in a vacuum. Though an occasional Jane Austen or Emily Dickinson seems but dimly related to the events of the time, most authors are the products of their age and would have written different works had they lived in another century. For example, Shakespeare's wide range is a personalized reflection of the Renaissance ideal of the universal man, and his experimentation with language was a characteristic of his day; his education, even though the learned Jonson saw fit to refer to his "small Latin and less Greek," was the typical classical education for bright boys of his time; his conversations at the Mermaid Tavern, his membership in a company of players, and his business dealings show that he was not secluded from life.

To understand an author well—despite the protestations of those critics who prefer to look solely at an undated anonymous text as an entity existing in and for itself alone—one should know something about his age, as we have already intimated: about its major historical events, about the cultural climate of the time, about what was happening in literature, art, music, architecture, science. Even what was happening in landscape gardening: the eighteenth century was a battleground for proponents of formal, straight-line, geometrical gardening and their adversaries who preferred curving, natural lines; their battle was related to the literary struggle between formal Neoclassicists and the gropers toward Romanticism who despised excessive restraint.

So reading in history is desirable for an English teacher. A smattering of political, economic, and military history is fine, but cultural and intellectual history is especially important. Unfortunately, too many college history courses still concentrate on dates and battles and elections, which are but surface eruptions suggesting faintly what was occurring underneath, like the lava pushed out the top of a volcano by invisible forces far below. But in some places there are history courses that probe deep and that consider the lives of people who were neither soldiers nor politicians. And, of course, there are books to be read, the modern descendants of Green's *History of the English People* or Traill and Mann's *Social England*.

The Bible, studied as literature, has significance to the teacher of literature. English and American literature abound in Biblical allusions. It is no accident that Jim Casy's initials, in *The Grapes of Wrath*, are the initials of Jesus Christ.

Mythology, too, has value and is not completely obsolete. The reader of Shakespeare, Milton, and a host of others is handicapped if he knows nothing of the Greek and Roman gods and goddesses and the legends associated with them and their subordinates. Their names survive in Venus pencils, Atlas tires (or a highway atlas), Mercury and Apollo spacecraft.

A knowledge of folklore is invaluable. Folklore is in part the literature of the folk: their tall tales, their riddles, their songs, their gusty and gutsy humor, their language play. Through folklore, students can realize that literature is not the private possession of bespectacled, college-bred men and women but also represents the pleasure that the earthbound often obtain from telling or hearing a story, singing a song, using language in untutored but often surprisingly effective ways.

The superior teacher is also versed in theories of literary criticism. Not because he will directly teach the theories, but because he will often apply them. Sometimes the explication favored by the "new" critics will help him and a class understand a difficult poem. Sometimes the application of psychological or historical or genre criticism will clear up a difficulty. Archetypal criticism will point toward other works with similar

44

themes or toward human characteristics deeply rooted in the past.

One more kind of background should be mentioned. Literature is a medium of communication. As such, it is related to other media: television, radio, movies, newspapers, magazines, advertising. We teachers like to believe that literature is supreme among the media, but admittedly it is not the most popular nor the best loved: a single television program may attract thirty million rapt viewers, but it is doubtful that Robert Frost had thirty million readers (outside the classroom) in his whole life. The secret of the appeal of other media should be a study of the teacher, for perhaps he can learn something to make literature more appealing to more people. Even if that does not prove true, the other media are important parts of the daily lives of his students and their parents, and if he is not to be a foreigner in their society, he must know much of what they enjoy and value and learn from.

The Intensive Reading of Literature

Though time-consuming, an independent in-depth reading of a single literary work is one of the most valuable exercises that a prospective teacher can perform. Ideally, there should be many such readings, but pressures of clock and calendar may prevent more than a few. Intensive reading supplemented by extensive reading related to a work can reveal processes invaluable in the teaching of literature, even though in a high school class no more than one or two or three of the processes may be employed.

Suppose that Keats' "Ode on a Grecian Urn" is the choice. (Any reputable work, prose or poetry, may be selected, if it has been the subject of numerous critical treatments.) The prospective teacher reads the ode, not just once or twice, but three, five, ten times, silently sometimes and aloud sometimes. He reads with mind alert, questioning. Who is the speaker? What is the situation? What is the mood? What is the author's apparent intention? What is his method?

He tries to visualize. If a single urn served as Keats' model (though in reality it may not have), how large was it? What was its probable shape? Were the figures painted or in bas-relief? What figures are presented? Where do they appear to be in relation to each other? How are they dressed? Are the altar and the little town of the fourth stanza portrayed on the urn? An understanding of imagery depends upon visualizing. (There is also an imagery of sound, feeling, even sometimes of taste and smell.)

He tries to understand the "hard words" and the allusions and the syntax: What is an "unravished bride of quietness," a "foster-child of silence and slow time," a "sylvan historian," "the sensual ear," "a heart high-sorrowful and cloyed," a "Cold Pastoral"? What is the definition of *loth, pipes, timbrels, heifer, attitude, brede, overwrought, waste*? What do the allusions to *Tempe* and to *Arcady* signify, and what was an *Attic* shape? What is the syntax of "All breathing human passion far above" and "not a soul to tell/Why thou art desolate, can e'er return"? Why does Keats use archaic diction: *thou, ye, say'st,* etc.?

He examines the structures of the five stanzas, noting the vocative or apostrophe that opens the poem and Keats' reiteration of the technique of direct address in other stanzas. He sees that the first vocative is followed by a series of questions addressed to the "sylvan historian." In the second stanza the speaker philosophizes about heard and unheard melodies, urges the pipes to continue their piping, and addresses and advises the "Bold Lover." In the third stanza, still using the vocative device, he addresses in turn the "happy boughs," the "happy melodist," and the "more happy, happy love." In the fourth stanza he asks questions of the "mysterious priest" and tells the "little town" that its streets will ever be silent. The last stanza addresses the entire urn and summarizes what the speaker believes is its message: "Beauty is truth, truth beauty." The structured analysis has revealed that in this poem Keats has used basically the technique of direct address, weaving the "message" into the one-sided conversations.

The teacher also looks into the prosody. The poem consists of five ten-line stanzas, rhyming ababcdedce or a slight variant, and the teacher tries to decide whether there is reason for the variations. The rhymes are not always perfect, at least in modern pronunciation: *unheard* and *endeared, sacrifice* and *skies, priest* and *dressed, morn* and *return, Pastoral* and *all*. Does this fact represent changes in pronunciation or sloppiness or conscious design? Each line is basically iambic pentameter, but there are many irregularities. Why do the irregularities exist? Do they strengthen the poem? Is there any pattern in the irregularities? What devices has Keats used to speed up or slow down the movement of lines? What other poetic devices has he used?

The teacher tries to pull parts together and encounters a few small or large puzzles. Is he sure, for instance, about the meaning of "Heard melodies are sweet, but those unheard/Are sweeter?" How should the line "Pipe to the spirit ditties of no tone" be read, and what are the "ditties" and what does "no tone" mean? Why did Keats mingle revelry and religion, as represented by the near-bacchanal and the "pious morn" of religious sacrifice? What are the implications of "Beauty is truth, truth beauty"? How suitable is the form to the content? What fundamentally is Keats saying in the poem? Most important, what does the poem say to me?

Note that so far the teacher has concentrated on the poem itself, separated from the rest of the universe. A good reader's first allegiance is to the work of art apart from any context. He tries to grasp it in itself.

But then, despite the adjurations of the "new" critics (now old or dead), he looks outside the poem for further enlightenment. He discovers, for one thing, that texts disagree about quotation marks in the final two lines of the last five:

> When old age shall this generation waste,
> Thou shalt remain, in midst of other woe,
> Than ours, a friend to man, to whom thou say'st,
> Beauty is truth, truth beauty,—that is all
> Ye know on earth, and all ye need to know.

Some editions use no quotation marks, others place the final two lines in quotes, and still others have quotes around only "Beauty is truth, truth beauty." What are the differences in meaning? Which version do textual scholars regard as authentic or at least best?

In looking at other critical treatments, he happens upon Gilbert Highet's "Keats's Greek Ode" in his *The Powers of Poetry*.[1] He discovers that Highet has found an urn that may have been Keats' inspiration—though other critics have other theories. More important, Highet is concerned with the pairing of revelry and religion in the ode and goes back to Nietzsche, who explains that "the civilization of the Greeks was a difficult tension, an almost irreconcilable conflict" between the life of reason and the "dark forces of the passions." "Therefore their

---

[1] (New York: Oxford University Press, 1960).

47

life, and most of their best art, were a continuous battle between the power which they personified as Bacchus or Dionysus—the deity who drives men and women into the wilds, whose servants are savage animals, whose rituals are close to madness—and the power they called Apollo, the god of reason, vision, and healing." The teacher considers this explanation not merely appealing and convincing but useful in a discussion of the poem. Not only the Greeks, he believes, were subject to such a conflict; all men and women are, all students are. Here is a clue for relating the poem to twentieth-century American lives, a clue for teaching self-understanding, an explanation of many of the contradictions in modern behavior that are otherwise inexplicable.

He reads also what other critics have said about Keats' thesis that life is short, but art is long, and traces this thesis back through Chaucer to Hippocrates. In pedagogical articles he finds how other teachers have tried to clarify this concept for their students. They have, for instance, talked about photographs as a means of catching the fleeting present moment for future enjoyment or the use of recordings to capture for centuries to come the magnificent voice of Caruso or the inspired performance of a Basin Street jazz combo.

He thinks about the application, to this poem, of Purves and Rippere's work.[2] They classify reactions to literature under the categories of Engagement-Involvement, Perception, Interpretation, and Evaluation. The teacher finds that with his knowledge of the poem he can write numerous statements under each heading, and he can thus clarify for himself some of the insights he hopes to develop later in student-readers.

He may also move out from the poem in other directions, each revelatory in its own way. Keats' "Endymion" confirms the poet's preoccupation with beauty: "A thing of beauty is a joy for ever:/ Its loveliness increases." Other poems reveal other facets of the intense young poet, and Keats' letters provide additional glimpses of his inner life, which may be supplemented by a biography for the outward details. And since Keats, like any other writer, was a product of his age, reading

---

[2] Alan C. Purves with Victoria Rippere, *Elements of Writing about a Literary Work: A Study of Response to Literature,* NCTE Research Report No. 9 (Champaign, Ill.: National Council of Teachers of English, 1968).

in the other Romantics and in the intellectual and cultural history of the time offers additional enlightenment.

The kind of reading recommended here obviously requires many hours and weeks and cannot be accomplished for large numbers of works. But it is worth the effort, because it can provide kinds of literary insight obtainable in no other way. Too many professors, influenced by the urge to "cover" a period or a genre, move rapidly across the surface with only an occasional dip beneath. The kind of reading we recommend can supplement and enrich any course and can also be done independently of a course. A splendid way to spend a summer!

Other Literary Experiences

"I don't like to read nothin' but football stories," the boy said.

"Sports stories are fine," said his teacher. "You've probably read most of the good ones about football, though. Do you like any other sports?" She was thumbing through a file of cards.

"Yeah. Basketball's okay. An' hockey. Baseball's not bad. But football's best."

"Let's see. John Tunis writes stories I think you'd like. *Yea! Wildcats!* is a basketball story that a lot of boys enjoy, and *Schoolboy Johnson* is about a rookie baseball pitcher. I don't know as much about athletics as I'd like to. I wish you'd read two or three about different sports and let me know if there's one that would reduce my ignorance a little. You mentioned hockey. I have cards here about Richard Flood's *Penalty Shot* and C. P. and O. B. Jackson's *Puck Grabber*. I know very little about hockey. Maybe you'd like to tell me what you think of one of them."

The boy slowly moved from football to other sports and then to stories about exploration. These interested him, unpredictably, in books on prospecting, which led him into geology. He never became excited about "literature" as teachers define it, but by the time he was a senior his reading horizon had broadened appreciably, and he read more books, on varied subjects, than he had ever read before.

The prospective teacher cannot possibly be intimately familiar with the vast range of books written for adolescents, but he should have browsed enough in them to be aware of what they offer, and he should not look upon them with contempt; some of the books, like Jack Schaefer's *Shane* and Esther Forbes' *Johnny Tremain*, are classics of their kind. Although most of what is read in a high school class should be "literature" in the traditional sense of the word (though selected with the interests and needs of the students constantly in mind), wide out-of-class reading in books for adolescents should be encouraged, and the teacher should be armed with knowledge about books that can gradually lead each child toward more mature reading materials. Some children, of course, are ready for the mature much earlier than others.

Many helps are available for the teacher. A course in literature for adolescents will introduce such annotated lists as the NCTE *Your Reading* (junior high level) and *Books for You* (senior high); it will give an opportunity to skim scores of books, to start a card file for future reference, and to discuss the relating of outside reading to in-class work. In the absence of such a course, the teacher can still secure copies of annotated lists and can read and keep for reference Dwight L. Burton's *Literature Study in the High Schools*.[3]

The literature of American minority groups has until recently been given too little attention. Some American literature textbooks have scarcely acknowledged that Negroes write, often very well, that there is sometimes the poetry of deep feeling in the language of the Navajos and other Indian tribes, that there are fine books by and about Puerto Ricans and Mexicans. Why should a Negro Catholic almost always be expected to read about the lives and the emotions of white Anglo-Saxon Protestants? He has a life, too, and emotions.

So, somewhere in the busy life of the teacher or teacher-to-be there should be found a little time to become familiar with people in heritages not his own. If he is white, he should read books like Richard Wright's *Black Boy* and *Native Son*, Langston Hughes' autobiographical *Not without Laughter*, much of James Baldwin, the poetry of Gwendolyn Brooks, even pitcher Bob Gibson's *From Ghetto to Glory;* and Negro magazines, including those of vehement protest. Regardless of his color, he should read books like Laura Hobson's *Gentlemen's Agreement* (on Jewish-Gentile relationships), Joseph Krumgold's *And Now, Miguel* (about Spanish-American sheep farmers), Miguel Covarrubias' *Mexico South* or Alice Blackwell's *Some*

---

[3] (New York: Holt, Rinehart and Winston, Inc., 1964).

Spanish-American Poets or Frances Toor's *Treasury of Mexican Folkways*, and Oliver La Farge's sensitive books about Indians.

Some professors of English, immersed in the Renaissance or the eighteenth century, may feel that reading of the sort described in this section is a waste of time, that the limited hours and weeks available should be devoted exclusively to the admittedly great. The great should have a degree of priority, true. But a high priority must be given also to human understanding of children and their heritage, of their concerns and problems, of the environment in which they live, of the tensions in modern society. Robert Browning still speaks to us, but so do James Baldwin and Ralph Ellison.

In the long run it is people who count—not words on a page or prosody or plot structure or archetypes. The teacher of literature must always remember that literature is about people, about him, about his students, about their ancestors and his, about future hopes and dreams. Wisely read and wisely taught, it can help move man toward greater compassion through greater understanding. The more the teacher knows about literature *as one of the humanities*, the greater his contribution to that goal.

4

Minimal	Good	Superior
An understanding of the place of oral communication in the teaching of English	An understanding of the principles of group discussion, group dynamics, panel discussions, classroom dramatizations, and choral reading; an understanding of the relationships between speaking and other facets of English	In addition to the "good" competencies: touches of expertise and showmanship that a professional speaker, oral interpreter, or actor possesses
An awareness of the role of listening in communication	A knowledge of current information relative to listening techniques	
An ability to speak with clarity and in conformity with present standards of educated usage	An ability to speak clearly and effectively, and in conformity with present standards of educated usage; an ability to recognize the virtues of divergence in language	
An ability to read aloud well enough for ready comprehension	An ability to read aloud well enough to convey most aspects of the interpretive art—meaning, mood, dominant emotions, varying emotions, overtones, and variety	

Knowledge and Skill
in Oral Communication

The Importance of Oral Communication in the English Classroom

We are concerned here not with formal speaking, debate, dramatic readings, or the performance of a school play. Nor are we concerned with speech correction, a highly technical subject that an amateur should not dabble with because of possibly serious consequences. We are discussing, rather, the role of speech in the English classroom and the special knowledge and skill of the English teacher in oral composition. Formal speaking and the rest should be left to the speech teacher.

There is much that the English teacher may do in the classroom with oral language. As linguists have been reminding us for two or three decades, language is primarily spoken, with written language a derivative. The human race talked for thousands of years before anything resembling writing was developed. Small children, too, speak long before they write, and as a rule those who are most orally articulate become the best readers and writers.

In their concern for improving writing, however, many teachers largely bypass oral communication. Their class discussions are little more than question-and-answer sessions or "recitations." In a study of many of the best high schools in the country, Squire and Applebee found only 19.3 percent of the class time devoted to discussion and 14.3 percent to student presentations, but 22.2 percent devoted to recitation and 21.1 percent to lecture.[1]

In 1965 a special NCTE task force reported on language programs for the disadvantaged. One of their ten major recommendations was the following:

> The lack of planned attention to oral pattern practice, to communicating ideas aloud, and to planned experiences in listening is a serious deficiency in many programs. Rigidly structured reading programs, without oral experiences using new vocabulary and sentence patterns, seem unlikely to achieve lasting growth.

---

[1] James R. Squire and Roger K. Applebee, *High School English Instruction Today* (New York: Appleton-Century-Crofts, 1968), p. 45.

The NCTE Task Force recommends that oral language receive greater stress in language instruction for the disadvantaged at all levels of education, from preschool through adult.

Only as progress is made in the use of oral language will there be substantial improvement in reading and writing. The interdependence of these language skills has been demonstrated both in research and in practice. All forms of drama, from puppetry to formal acting, and the oral tradition of literature need to be given greater emphasis in schools.[2]

John Dixon, in writing about the Dartmouth Seminar, said: "In English, pupils meet to share their encounters with life, and to do this effectively they move freely between dialogue and monologue—between talk, drama, and writing." [3]

In short, the guiding of experience in oral communication is a significant task of the teacher of English, though he shares this responsibility with the teacher of speech and, to some extent, with all other teachers. But since the use of language as an instrument for sending and receiving communications is a central concern of English, the English teacher must make sure that adequate and appropriate opportunities for such use are made available in his classroom.

The British Emphasis

In the past few years, British teachers of English have moved far in the direction of increased oral emphasis. Pantomime and improvisation and classroom drama are frequent, and class discussions on topics of genuine interest to the children are a way of life. Concerning the latter, Dixon has this to say:

Whenever English is based on first-hand experience and real life a teacher needs to look hard at the role he can best fill. Generally the focus of his attention is on the experience and how to elicit a fuller understanding of it. Where, then, does he turn his attention to the *manner* of speaking? Surely with the need for a presentation of findings to a group of classmates, the entire class, or a still larger part of the school community. Effective speech is learnt not in front of audiences who are only to be conjured in the imagination—the dummy run approach—but in preparation for saying something of significance to real audiences. When a class works in groups—on the language of advertisements, say—a simple presentation by each

---

[2] Richard Corbin and Muriel Crosby, cochairmen, *Language Programs for the Disadvantaged* (Champaign, Ill.: National Council of Teachers of English, 1965), pp. 272–273.

[3] *Growth through English* (Reading, England: National Association for the Teaching of English, 1967), p. 13.

group is natural and inevitable. When the class as a whole have found a theme that inspired them, or produced a radio ballad, this is a natural thing to present in school assembly. In such circumstances a limited conception of what is involved will produce failure; as Alexander Frazier notes, the teacher cannot "settle for judgments made according to such questions as these: Did the speaker stand up straight? Look us in the eye? Make any errors in grammar? Say AH or ER between sentences?" A pupil might "fail" on nearly all these minor points and still successfully challenge his audience to respond to what he had to say. . . . "It is through . . . talk that children can best find out in exchange with one another what are their responses to an experience, real or symbolic, and help one another to come to terms with it. Such talk does not occur in the classroom, however, without deliberate design; it is most likely when small groups of pupils talk about matters which engage their deepest attention. Nor will children talk in this way unless they feel that their responses and opinions are valued, and this has implications for the teacher's relationship with his pupils. Works of literature enter this talk as voices contributing to the conversation, and the talk in its turn provides a context for literature, which helps the children to take in what the voices have to say." ([Douglas] Barnes)[4]

So the British place much stress on discussions and informal reports (or "monologues," as they sometimes call them). The discussions sometimes involve small groups, sometimes the whole class. The teacher is the catalyst, the "father of the feast," but seldom dominates, though he often steps in to shorten tangents that are straying too far, or to provide a relevant or essential bit of information, or to build a bridge to what should come next. The class atmosphere is almost always friendly and cooperative, often excited, very often controversial. The subject matter varies but frequently derives from literature being read. The discussions are more mature in quality in the upper forms, partly because the children are older, but partly because through experience they have learned to distinguish evidence from opinion, to avoid name-calling and card-stacking and the other devices of the propagandist, and to respect the opinions of others even when they disagree. Good discussions, in England or in America, are a far cry from teacher-ask student-answer.

The word *oracy* (a parallel to *literacy*) does not appear in Webster III, but British teachers often refer to it. Their responsibility, they believe, is not merely that of helping children achieve literacy—familiarity with the written or printed word— but also that of helping them attain oracy, the effective sending

---

[4] *Ibid.*, pp. 35–36.

and receiving of oral communication. *Oracy* is a useful word; maybe it will be in Webster IV.

Pantomime and improvisation are other favored British devices. A class of twelve-year-olds, divided into groups, pantomime common household tasks like making tea, or after reading a story about coal-mining they pantomime some key scenes. A group of fifteen-year-olds improvise the conversation when a boy informs his family and his girl friend that he is planning to quit school and take a job; it's not quite *commedia dell'arte,* but both cast and audience learn from it. A group of boys recreate in their own language a scene from *Julius Caesar,* and after some conversation the class decides that maybe Shakespeare did say it a little better but didn't have any more fun.

They write plays, radio shows, and movie scripts and sometimes make movies. (One class, limited by money to two hundred feet of film, spent hours in detailed planning of the story line so as not to waste one precious foot. They probably learned more about composing than most classes learn in a year.) They get inside the characters. Through participation in the making of literature with a small l they learn much about Literature with a big L. Dixon says,

> Pupils of fourteen to eighteen learn to change and reverse roles, to see the situation from many perspectives, and—in the writing of scripts—to use the many voices of the "characters" to build within themselves an image of the complexity of the world as they know it.[5]

James Moffett, an American, continues the argument in favor of high priority for drama and dramatizing in the school program:

> Drama is the most accessible form of literature for young and uneducated people. It is made up of action; and the verbal action is the sort we practice all the time. A kindergarten child or an older illiterate can soliloquize and converse, verbalize to himself and vocalize to others. No written symbols are required. Drama is primitive: not only does it hit us at the level of sensation, affect, and conditioned response, but it seems in all cultures to be virtually the first, if not the first, verbal art to come into being, because it is oral and behavioral and functional, evolving directly out of real-life activities, such as propitiating gods, making rain, and girding for war.[6]

Some British classrooms aren't as orderly as orderly teachers and orderly administrators may like in their orderly schools.

---

[5] *Ibid.,* p. 39.

[6] *Drama: What Is Happening* (Champaign, Ill.: National Council of Teachers of English, 1967), p. 3.

There's a great deal of talk—sometimes loud talk—and a great deal of laughter and groups rehearsing and six things happening at once. And the discussions aren't always on sterilized topics, and the plays often aren't sterilized either. (Nor other literature. One of the two most discussed writers in the upper forms is D. H. Lawrence.) The talk and the drama may be about anything, even alcohol, narcotics, and S-E-X. (An American professor was asked in a class of British fifteen-year-old girls, "Do they have the pill in America?" "Yes." "Does your wife use them?" This is known as British reserve.)

This Side of the Water

Many American teachers would not feel at ease in such uninhibited surroundings. But even though they may not go all-out with the oral emphasis, as a large number of British teachers do, many American teachers spend considerable time in genuine discussion of topics that have no pat answers, and they make much use of panels, symposiums, and individual reports that the class is really eager to hear. Less attention now to the report for the sake of a report: "I want each of you to be ready tomorrow to talk for three minutes on the eighteenth-century coffee houses." Less attention now to the stultified book report: "Start with the title, author, and setting, identify the main characters, and then . . ." More attention to issues, to problems, to enlightenment of others concerning a subject that one has recently learned about and found fascinating. More interplay of words and ideas among the students. More teacher-fading-into-background.

Growing up is a process of becoming independent. The baby is weaned from the nursing bottle, learns to like solid food, soon is raiding the refrigerator by himself, and eventually as an adult puts food into the refrigerator and doesn't just take it out. Mama's apron strings have gradually been taken away. So should the school's apron strings be removed. The child learns to become independent by being independent. Too rigid structuring, too close guidance of every child's response, delays maturation. Perhaps half of college failures result from insufficient ability of students—young men and women—to stand on their own feet, to be self-disciplined and independent. Oversolicitous parents and teachers have controlled too many minutes of too many days. Children have been told too often what to think and have been given too little opportunity to think. Speech is oral thought. It is a tool for building independence.

British students in schools emphasizing oracy don't groan when they are asked to write. Many American students do. British students in experimental schools don't groan when they are asked to read a poem, or a play by Shakespeare. Many American students do. The British associate writing and reading with the discussions and the dramatizations in class, which provide fuel for writing what one believes in and is excited about; and the reading provides more fuel for further discussion. The separation of the "language arts" is a false separation. They work together, each reinforcing the others.

Children listen when there is a good reason for listening. What child won't listen carefully when someone says, "For your birthday I'm thinking about getting you some . . ."? Skills of listening can be taught more easily with a carrot than with a stick. One kind of carrot is lively discussion in which each student at any moment may be expected to contribute, rebut, agree, or supplement. The teacher should know how to bring out this carrot and others. The classroom goal should not be a series of dialogues—teacher and one student, teacher and another student, and so on in the age-old pattern of recitation. And certainly the goal should not be what Abraham Kaplan of the University of Michigan calls a "duologue," in which "everybody talks and nobody listens," and which "takes place in schools, churches, cocktail parties, the U.S. Congress and almost everywhere we don't feel free to be wholly human." Instead, the objective should be a "polylogue," in which each person has an opportunity to speak and in which everyone else listens and has a chance to react.

What kind of college preparation is desirable for the English teacher as a teacher of oral communication? The midnight conversations in the dormitory probably contribute more than any course. In those sessions the college students wrestle with questions of timeless concern as well as questions of the immediate present: Is there a God? How can wars be prevented? What is morality? How can you win a girl (or a boy)? To what extent should students control their curriculum requirements? Is Professor X fair in his grading? Who will win Saturday's game? In such discussions, on topics ranging from God to game, no holds are barred. Anything goes. Extreme positions may be taken. People sometimes play roles, including that of devil's advocate. The search is less for victory than for ever-elusive truth. People listen to one another, respond to one another. If discussion departs too far from the subject, someone usually drags it back. Such midnight-oil discussions are closely akin to good discussions in the secondary school classroom.

An elementary course in public speaking may develop in the prospective teacher some self-assurance about appearing before a group, though in its worst guise it holds the danger of confirming the belief that education consists of telling: many a teacher-lecturer got started along his evil path when he earned an A in Speech 100. In its ideal form, Speech 100 engrains truths about organization and delivery and discussion; if so, it proves later to be of constant value in the classroom.

Of undeniable value is a course in oral interpretation of literature. A group of English teachers polled in an ISCPET study voted overwhelmingly that the ability to read aloud effectively was one of the most important skills. The voice and body can communicate the meaning of a literary work. What otherwise might be little more than a grouping of words on a page becomes an integrated piece of art, with a life and vigor of its own. Speech is not separated from literature: a thorough understanding of the literary text must precede any effective oral interpretation. The quality, pitch, rate, and force of the presentation depend upon an understanding of the purpose, mood, and style of the literary work. The voice needs to suggest not only the denotative but also the connotative values of words. Syntactic difficulties are reduced by the speaker's emphasis on key words. The oral reader becomes a go-between for the literary work and the audience, translating one for the other. He makes literature live.

The satisfactory course in oral interpretation emphasizes solo reading but incorporates other elements: book talks and book reviews (with excerpts read), storytelling and perhaps a lecture recital, and group performances including reader's theatre ("involving delineated characters with or without a narrator and with focus placed off stage"), chamber theatre (which "stages prose fiction without rewriting the text, keeping the narrative form, and placing the scenes on stage"), and choral reading ("an ensemble activity using voices in unison or in antiphonal or solo arrangements"). All these activities can later be transferred to the secondary classroom, where the teacher sometimes "performs" but more often leads his students into their own oral interpretations. British children, for example, read a play as a play, not as a classroom exercise; they take parts, read them well or badly, sometimes reread them, talk about what they have read, perhaps go through a scene several times. And they learn much more than if they had merely analyzed, picked out the similes, and talked about the characters as mere names on a page.

In connection with his own oral use of language, a prospective teacher needs to learn to live comfortably in an area between careless, sloppy, anything-goes language and the excessive preciseness or prissiness of "schoolmarm English." Like if he finds himself like using *like* like seven times in two sentences, he may suspect that a bit of moderation is desirable. Or if he says *can't never* and *each of them are,* he is somewhat deaf and blind to the usage of most present-day educated Americans. Or if he mumbles, and swallows his word endings, and frequently is asked "Wadjasay?" he probably should make a tape recording of one of his conversations and listen to himself. (A classroom teacher, too, can sometimes profit from recording an hour of discussion with his class and then listening to himself—to note both whether he talks too much and whether what he says is distinct.) On the other hand, he is no better off if he is so extremely puristic that he never splits an infinitive, if he says "For what are you waiting?" instead of the more natural "What are you waiting for?" and if he pronounces ev-e-ry syllable with unhuman meticulousness. His goal should be to use his language orally in comfortable conformity with the everyday, nonplatform custom of the majority of twentieth-century educated Americans.

In relation to the language of his students, somewhere a prospective teacher should learn something that, regrettably, many experienced teachers have never learned: divergence of language in the classroom has its virtues. A class that has speakers of several geographical dialects is more fortunate than one in which everyone possesses the same accent and lexicon; the dialects offer spice, reflect some of the diversity of America, and help in building essential awareness of language characteristics that otherwise might be only words in a regional novel. And some students who speak a not universally approved social dialect may express themselves with vigor and vividness alien to students from "better" environments. Students may learn much from one another's language, but not in a classroom where there is unbending insistence upon complete conformity, and certainly not in a classroom in which anyone's language—an intimate possession—is ridiculed and treated as an inferior, almost worthless thing.

Somewhere, too, the teacher-to-be must learn as much as possible about the mass media, the mass-media machines that, as McLuhan repeatedly insists, are beginning to affect our age as profoundly as the invention of movable type affected the last five hundred years. Our children have grown up with television and with movies, with seeing-hearing and not just reading. They know tape recorders and intercoms and overhead projectors and perhaps computerized instruction where they "converse" with a machine. Though the English teacher's first love may well remain the printed and the spoken word, there must be knowledge of these other forces that shape students' lives. Tapes and videotapes can be used in the classroom. A movie or a TV program can sometimes clarify the unclear. Impromptu sketches on a transparency can accompany a presentation, and a series of prepared overlays can explain a difficult point in language. The media can often be related to work in the classroom. As Mary Columbro Rodgers says:

> Students need exercise in handling the *content* of the mass media as well as the media itself. High level integration can be effected when programs viewed at home become the subject matter of other English-related exercises. For example, the key factors in short fiction can be taught as efficiently in relation to television drama as to prose fiction. In class discussions, many students can refer to a variety of programs, thus enriching the English lesson. Children see little relationship between their school subjects and their many hours of television consumption. The English teacher might well serve an important role in helping children synthesize their total verbal experiences by integrating out-of-class popular art with in-class English experiences.[7]

The English teacher is not expected to become a professional speaker or actor. Nevertheless, his knowledge of the potential values of the human voice and his own skill in using his voice can be of immense value to him in the classroom. Although he may not, like some British teachers, favor an oracy-centered school, oracy does have importance to his students now and in the years when they will no longer be students.

---

[7] *New Design in the Teaching of English* (Scranton, Pa.: International Textbook Co., 1968), p. 83.

5

Minimal	Good	Superior
A knowledge and appreciation of students as individuals		
Creative approaches to meeting the social responsibility of teaching English to all youth		
Some understanding of basic principles of educational psychology	Knowledge of educational psychology, especially of the learning process and adolescent psychology	Competence in the knowledge and application of educational psychology; detailed knowledge of the stages of growth in children and youth
Introductory knowledge of American secondary education	Knowledge of the philosophy, organization, and educational programs of American secondary education now and in historical perspective	
A basic understanding of the content, instructional materials, and organization of secondary English programs	A good understanding of the content, instructional materials, and organization of secondary English programs, and of the role of English in the total school program	A thorough understanding of the content, instructional materials, and organization of secondary English programs, and of the role of English in the total school program; knowledge of principles of curriculum development in English
A basic knowledge of ways to teach English, with an awareness of the importance of developing assignments that guide students in their study of language, written and oral communication, and literature	A wide knowledge of effective ways to teach English, to select and adapt methods and materials for the varying interests, environments, abilities, and maturity levels of students, and to develop a sequence of assignments to guide and stimulate students in their study of language, written and oral communication, and literature	A thorough knowledge of the most effective ways to teach English, to select and adapt methods and materials for the varying interests and maturity levels of students, and to develop sequential assignments that guide, stimulate, and challenge students in their study of language, written and oral communication, and literature
Some knowledge of corrective and developmental reading techniques	Moderate knowledge of corrective and developmental reading techniques	A relatively thorough knowledge of corrective and developmental reading techniques
A basic understanding of the uses of mass media and multi-media approaches in the teaching of English	Knowledge of ways to select and use mass media and multi-media approaches to enhance the teaching of English	Sophistication concerning the selection and use of mass media and multi-media approaches to enrich the teaching of English
Understanding of basic principles of evaluation and test construction in English	Broad understanding of basic principles of evaluation and test construction in English	Thorough understanding of basic principles of evaluation and test construction in English

Knowledge and Skill
in the Teaching of English

Why Take "Education"?

The classroom is almost the payoff. (Not quite, for the real payoff for high school students comes after they have taken their last formal course and are working at their diverse jobs, raising families, participating in their own ways in their own segment of society. And since that's the real payoff for students, it is for the teacher, too—what happens to each of these kids-become-adults, partly as a result of his teaching.) The classroom is what the teacher is being prepared for. Parents and other taxpayers pay him mainly for what he does in the classroom. Here is the setting, usually, for modest success or modest failure; occasionally, for major success or major failure.

What the teacher knows about his subject contributes much to his success, and that hard-to-define quality known as personality makes its contribution, and so do such other qualities as genuine interest in young people, dedication—a whole catalog of virtues that no one can possess in full unless he is able to walk on water. But beyond the knowledge and skills that we have discussed in earlier chapters, and beyond "personality" and "virtues," there is one more ingredient. The teacher should know about the classroom, the things that have gone on and can go on in classrooms, the theory and practice of teaching and learning—especially the teaching and learning of English. Courses in education are included in teacher-preparatory programs because, at their best, they provide enlightenment about students, about classes, and about interaction—between student and student, student and teacher, student and teacher and subject, student and teacher and the school environment, student and teacher and the human community.

Basic Knowledge of Education

Most states require for teacher certification some courses in general psychology, educational or child or adolescent psychology, and history and philosophy of education. Only occasionally are such courses among students' favorites, but potentially they are very valuable, and in the hands of the most able professors their value is constantly demonstrated.

The various kinds of courses in psychology, wisely taught, transcend rats and mazes and ganglia and statistics and research reports. They are humanized. From them the teacher-to-be can learn much about what makes people people. He can learn about human drives and ambitions, about the causes and preventives of frustration, about the basic emotions and their influences on every human moment. He can learn how children grow and develop physically and mentally, how the adolescent differs from the preadolescent, what it is that worries or inspires or frightens or consoles the child and the young person. He can find out what is known about the process of learning, what the theories of learning are; the English teacher can learn what little has been found out about how children acquire and develop language. The psychologies are not—or should not be—dryasdust study; they are—or should be—the best answers that present-day science can offer to age-old questions about the nature of man.

The history and philosophy of education can be relevant, too. Twentieth-century education is not a newly sprung plant. It has roots reaching deep into the past. For millenniums adults have sought the best ways to acquaint their children with what must be known and done for survival, and with the culture and the traditions of their people; even primitive societies have to educate their young. For millenniums people have groped for the most effective ways of teaching. They have found some ways that succeed, and they have made many mistakes. Modern teachers can profit from both the successes and the failures, if they know them. That is what the history of education is about.

The educational philosophers have been among the searchers. They often do not agree with one another, and that is well, because if all searchers followed the same path, the forest to the right and to the left would remain unexplored. They have not found the definitive answers, because the forest stretches far in all directions. But a teacher should know their tentative answers and some of the many questions that still elude the frontier thinkers and are the subject of their truth-seeking debates.

We began this book with a chapter about the child. The child is the primary concern of the required courses in education, or at least he ought to be. The child as he is and can become. The child with the poor neural connections and the one who thinks so rapidly as to seem almost intuitive, and the majority of children who are not close to either extreme. The child from the inner city, the wealthiest suburb, the farm away back in the hills on a winding clay road. The child with the dark skin as well as the one with a different pigmentation. (Around the world, Caucasians are a minority race.) The motivated child and the one who seems to care for nothing. The cautious and the bold. The boy and the girl. Every child. No two exactly alike. Each capable of performing in his lifetime something detrimental to human society, or something good for it.

That child is what education courses are about. The best professors never forget the child, even when they are considering abstruse theory or a statistical table. If a teacher-to-be has a professor who does forget, he himself should try as well as he can to visualize the children behind the words and the percentages.

Secondary School English Programs

Diploma in hand (or at any rate in a safe-deposit box or hanging in a frame in his parents' home), the clear-eyed young teacher one September morning appears before the first class that he can call his own. His mind is well stocked with knowledge of literature, language, and written and oral composition, and with what his courses in education have taught him about the child and the school. He has notebooks filled with gleanings from his college years.

In part his success in teaching during that first day and first year—indeed throughout his teaching career—will depend upon what he knows about secondary school English programs: what they contain, what materials are available, what organizational patterns are possible. Though his own ability to plan and to innovate is of high importance, he does not need to invent the wheel; somebody else did that long ago. And though he may be handed a curriculum or a curriculum guide or a detailed course of study, he should understand the principles upon which it is based and the possible directions in which he may depart from it when he comes to know the peculiar needs, interests, limitations, and strengths of his own students.

Through college class discussions, professional reading, and examination of courses of study, our clear-eyed young teacher has learned much of what experienced teachers have considered teachable, what their goals have been, and how they have organized the content and materials for their courses. He has not found agreement among these teachers, and the experience of some has contradicted that of others. He has not found a neat package that contains solutions for all problems. But he has found plans that have worked for some teachers and some schools and some children. He has at his disposal a range of applied theory, an array of possibilities. He has learned that everything from comic books to *Paradise Lost* has been taught with profit to children, that rich offerings in the English language have heightened children's language power, that a well-conceived composition program does indeed increase children's skill in writing.

He has examined the varied principles or theories of English curriculum design (described in the introduction): the communication theory, the tripod theory, the unified field theory, and so on. Tentatively, he has chosen the one that appeals most to him, or he may select from several and put parts together in a design that seems to him most viable. (He may change his mind later. Mental growth comes from change of mind; the stubborn who refuse to alter their opinions are locked forever in an unbreakable shell.) Knowing the existing theories can provide a basis for his thinking now and later; it will serve him well if he is content to rest on the theorizing of others or provide a point of departure if he is highly innovative.

Somewhere, too, the young teacher has learned about the wealth of materials available to the teacher of English. Books are of course primary, for a fundamental part of his job is to open with young people the covers of many books. In addition, though, he has learned how to find available films, videotapes, filmstrips, slides, tapes, recordings, programed instructional materials, microfilm and microfiche, transparencies, and whatever other useful materials the inventors bring across the horizon. Note that we said "how to find" these things. An educated man has been defined as a person who knows how to find whatever he wants. His mind need not be cluttered with thousands of titles and addresses, for it is the function of a catalog to hold such information until it is needed. But the teacher should know what and where the catalogs are, so that when he is planning to teach, say, *Hamlet* he will be able to discover quickly what films, recordings, or other materials can supplement and clarify the play and enrich students' understandings of it.

Materials are not all ready-made. Sometimes making is more valuable than using. Occasionally a class may learn much from making a short film of its own, or a tape recording, or some transparencies, and the teacher should be alert to such possibilities. He need not be a technician: there are always some students (maybe boys not much interested in anything else) who are eager to handle the mechanical gadgets. The teacher who sometimes lets a class compose in another medium may find a carryover to composing with words and to appreciation of other people's composing.

Back to a broader view: How is English related to the total school program? The young teacher has had a chance to think about this question. He realizes that in English classes the students get their most prolonged introduction to the humanities. Humanities deal with people and with what people may be and may become. They concern what is real and what is "such stuff as dreams are made on." They carry truth and they carry visions. Most other school subjects deal with the factual— the chief industries of New England, the structure of the oxygen atom, the causes of the Civil War, protection against venereal disease, how to play basketball, how to find the volume of a sphere. The factual and the humanistic (partly factual) are both important; they are not competitors or enemies. There should be no war with science on on side and arts and humanities on the other, for the well-educated need both. They complement each other. Tentacles of English reach out and draw from the sciences, and the best scientists draw inspirations from their knowledge of the humanities, trying to make chemistry and physics and astronomy the servants of man.

There has long been discussion, in both schools and colleges, of whether the English department is a service department for the others, of whether the English teacher's chief task is not instruction in reading and writing so that students can read their history and science texts and write papers as required in such courses. Most English teachers indignantly reject such a statement, and rightly so, since certainly their task transcends that lowly definition. Yet the role cannot be completely declined, for in a sense each department contributes in its own way to preparing students to do the best possible work in each other department. Thus mathematics serves the sciences in obvious ways, health instruction may help to develop and maintain the sound body that contains the sound mind which other departments seek, art and music contribute to the esthetic appreciation that literature teachers also desire, and history provides a context into which other knowledge may be fitted. English, as one part of its function, does indeed provide a service to other departments, and there should be pride rather than shame in announcing the fact. The role of English does not stop with such service but does include it, though basically the service is to the student rather than to another department, through helping him to learn to read and write as well as possible, throughout his life, in whatever sort of work he does.

Sometimes one hears the slogan "Every teacher a teacher of English," implying that every teacher in every department shares in the responsibility for developing literacy. Like many slogans, this one is composed of partial truth. It is false if it means that every teacher should teach sentence structure and punctuation and the organization of a paragraph, or if it means that he should red-pencil every faulty spelling or questionable usage. He may not be well enough informed to do such things, and he may object to usages that English teachers know are now standard; besides, he has his own important material to teach and should not be expected to take time away from the study of science and give it to the study of sentences. The slogan is true, however, if it is interpreted to mean that every teacher should do two things on behalf of English: (1) show steadily his belief that good English is important, through insisting that students always write and speak as clearly and well as they are able, and (2) teach the English skills implicit in his subject, such as the spelling and meaning of *hydrochloric* or the way to read a formula, graph, or technical paper in his own field.

Methodology

College courses in methods of teaching English and in student teaching, it must be realized, provide no more than an introduction and a preliminary apprenticeship. An alert teacher never assumes that he knows enough about how to teach, and he tries constantly to learn more.

Nevertheless, a specialized methods course and carefully supervised student teaching can contribute extensively to the prospective teacher's knowledge and skill. A general methods course, still the only one available in many small colleges, is likely to be of less value, since it must cater to the varied needs of the teacher of music, physical education, history, chemistry,

English, and other subjects and necessarily can go only into slight detail in any single field. Some of the small colleges, however, partially compensate by adding a one- or two-semester-hour special supplement for English; also, some particularly skilled general-methods professors are able to fashion special assignments highly valuable to the differing requirements of different subjects. The student teacher's college supervisor and his supervising teacher, combined with his firsthand experience with students in the classroom, can also acquaint the teacher-to-be with much that he needs to know about methodology.

Our statement concerning the "good" qualifications emphasizes the fact that methodology rises much above the level of gimmickry:

> A wide knowledge of effective ways to teach English, to select and adapt methods and materials for the varying interests, environments, abilities, and maturity levels of students, and to develop a sequence of assignments to guide and stimulate students in their study of language, written and oral communication, and literature

This implies, for example, that the teacher is aware of the values of inductive teaching and knows how to teach inductively, that he also knows when a different approach may be preferable, or that he can look at his teaching from the viewpoint suggested by the Flanders Interaction Analysis. It implies further that when he thinks about the content of the courses he teaches, he relates that content to his students; if he is going to teach *Great Expectations*, for instance, he does not plan a college-level treatment of that novel but instead plans ways to deal with it that are in keeping with the intellectual and maturational and emotional levels of his students. And it implies that he thinks not just of day-to-day assignments and objectives but also of sequence. An objective for today's assignment should be a part of and a contributor to a larger objective, but a beginning teacher sometimes becomes so engrossed in planning for today that he loses sight of tomorrow and the next day.

His methods course, then, should require him to prepare a variety of lesson plans but also plans for larger segments of work. The lesson plans include the objectives, materials, and procedures for specific lessons. Some of these should be in literature, some in written and oral communication, some in language, most in a combination of two or three of the elements. They should afford him the opportunity to bring in a number of diverse approaches that may be suggested by his methods text, his instructor, or his own independent reading and his imagination. His plans for larger segments, "units" as they are often called, should enable him to look at what he expects to drive toward over a period of weeks; ordinarily they should combine instruction in the various parts of English: literature, language, oral and written presentation. These parts are not rigidly separated in life and should not be separated in the classroom.

Methodology is a catalyst designed to encourage interaction between content and student. The teacher is attempting, for instance, to make a literary work an experience for his students, to engender within them a degree of understanding of the work and to get them to respond to it. Some methods are more effective than others in creating such interaction: one method may kill interest and another may make students eager to read more in the same author or the same genre. Similarly, in language study one method may cause students to believe that language is dull and uninteresting but another may lead them to the awareness that language is endlessly fascinating. Methodology, then, should not be despised or underrated. Though a knowledge of methods and techniques can never be substituted for solid knowledge of the subject, it can do much in bringing out in students the kinds of responses that English teachers constantly seek.

Reading

They enter the junior or senior high school, these students, able to read very well, able to struggle through a simple story, or hardly able to read at all. The random matings in the cave perhaps have something to do with their ability, and so do the accidents of neural connections or home environment or motivation or earlier teaching. The English teacher—as well as other teachers—has something to do with bringing each student's reading up to the highest level possible for that student, even though he cannot cancel out the past.

So the teacher should know a little bit about how reading is taught in the grades—look-and-say, phonics, alphabetic, or what-have-you. And the more he knows about each student, the better. Often a student's motivation to read has never been developed. If the teacher can find the keys to motivation (a single key will not open all doors), if he can get a student excited about reading or at least aware that reading can do something for him, even the nonreader may become a reader.

74

But sometimes the problem is too complex for the non-specialist. Sometimes only a reading clinic or a psychologist can be of much help. The teacher needs to recognize the signs so that he can refer some students to the specialist.

Within the classroom, though, there is much that the teacher can do to improve the reading of most students. The reading of literature is reading. Composition is reading in reverse: what is composed will supposedly be read by someone. Language study is related to reading, for it deals with symbols that must be interpreted. The teacher's preparation in literature, composition, and language has therefore given him much of what he needs as a teacher of reading. Reading is not just a process; one always reads something. He does not read *reading*.

In his attempts to help each student to read better, the high school English teacher concentrates on individual students' interests, attitudes, and abilities. He consciously and constantly tries to extend, broaden, and develop these interests and abilities, starting if necessary with *Hot Rod* and moving—rapidly or at snail's pace—to *The Secret Sharer*. He gives suggestions as needed concerning the techniques of reading appropriate for various purposes. The expository article read as background for a composition is not approached in the same way as a short story from *Seventeen* read for entertainment, and the reading of Poe's "The Raven" is not quite the same as the reading of Arnold's "Dover Beach," and both of these are read differently from *The Pearl* or "Chrysanthemums." The teacher helps students not only to select materials but also to establish varied purposes and realistic goals for reading. And always, through everything that goes on in the classroom, he adds experiences and concepts that will lead toward increased success and pleasure in attaining the goals.

The reading experts talk of such goals as using context clues for vocabulary, retaining details, organizing sequences of events and other relationships, discovering and interpreting main ideas and generalizations, criticizing, and appreciating. Such goals are obviously not alien to the study of literature and of language. When the teacher teaches literature and language well, he is teaching reading well. Students' responses to literary works are a measurement of their reading ability. And their ability to recognize words, analyze meanings, grasp the meaning relationships within a sentence, and observe how sentences fit together in paragraphs—indeed all components of language study have value in increasing comprehension.

Somewhere in the teacher's preparatory program, then, should be a practical, down-to-earth course that shows how the person who is not a reading specialist can, within the walls of his own classroom, develop the reading power of his students by making use of what he already knows about literature, composition, and language.

Measurement and Evaluation

"How am I doing?" the teacher asks himself frequently. "Am I getting the most I can from these students and this material? Have I planned well? Have I prepared adequately? Have I been stressing the consequential rather than the inconsequential, the important rather than the trivial? Am I alive and lively? Do I respect my students as a group and as individuals? Am I willing to listen to them or do I do most of the talking? Do I avoid the extremes of authoritarianism or so much permissiveness that my class is anarchic? Looking ahead, what further study and preparation do I need so that in future years I can do a still better job?"

"How are they doing?" the teacher also asks. "As a group, are my students increasing their ability to discuss, to respect their fellows even when they disagree? As a group, do they understand what our objectives are, and are they moving, though perhaps slowly, toward those objectives?"

"How is each student doing?" the teacher asks most often. *Each*, we have said before, is one of the most important words in the language, especially in teaching. Despite John Donne, to some extent each boy or girl, each man or woman, *is* an island: even when he mingles with his fellows and influences them and is influenced by them, each person lives inside his own skin and will always live there and will die inside his own skin, filled with personal regrets and memories of personal accomplishments.

Evaluation, a ceaseless process, constantly considers all three of these questions: How am I doing? How are they doing? How is each doing? It is thus much more than putting a grade on a paper or a report card.

Evaluation is not separated from teaching and learning. It is not an epilogue, an after-the-fact procedure. It is related both to the statement of objectives and to the activities of the course segment and the whole course. For example, when the teacher decides, or decides with the class, upon the basic objectives for teaching Knowles' *A Separate Peace*, he also thinks about or

76

even prepares evaluative procedures that will measure the degree of students' (and a student's) attainment of those objectives. In the process of teaching he may find it necessary to modify some of the objectives and consequently the means of evaluation, but nevertheless evaluation is built into the total act of teaching. Too many teachers, not realizing clearly that evaluation is part of a seamless garment, teach one thing and test another without ever realizing what they are doing; then they wonder why students do so poorly on their tests.

When teacher and class can decide together about objectives, it is not unreasonable to discuss also the means of measuring attainment. "How can we find out how well we're doing?" teacher and class ask. Certainly tests are not the only devices. Discussion, group or individual projects, compositions, and demonstrations are among the others. Sometimes the best measure of attainment is excited response by all or nearly all the students; sometimes it is only a quiet sentence spoken by a student to the teacher after class.

Since tests are always with us, though—since some sort of testing is in fact a frequent ingredient in almost everyone's life today—the teacher needs to know something about tests, how they are constructed, what kinds there are, what their virtues and limitations are. He should know, for instance, that tests have various purposes, including diagnosis (most school systems don't do enough diagnosing of individual needs), measurement of achievement, determining the possible desirability of re-teaching, screening of students for various purposes, and measurement of the effectiveness of instruction itself.

So the teacher ought to be familiar with kinds of tests and test questions. Robert Carruthers' *Building Better English Tests* (NCTE) is a good introduction to teacher-made tests. For broader coverage, Buros' *Sixth Mental Measurements Yearbook* (Gryphon Press), though much of it is irrelevant to English, provides an overview of possibilities, and Buros' *Tests in Print* (Gryphon Press) is a useful catalog.

Some of the jargon of the measurement people should be in his vocabulary, though certainly not all or even most of it. There is, for example, an important distinction between the *validity* and the *reliability* of a test item or a test. When the jargon is essential for making such distinctions, the teacher should know what it means to people who have devoted their lives to measurement.

Evaluation instruments, whether formal tests or something else, need to be balanced, fair, and relevant. The parts should be weighted so that a suitable amount of credit, based on importance in terms of learning, is given to each part. Too often we teachers have concocted unbalanced instruments simply because some things are easier to measure than other things; in literature, for instance, though we may have been stressing understanding of characters, we sometimes have constructed picky little test items on the level of "On which shoulder did Long John Silver's parrot sit?"

Writing down a grade on a report card is the most painful part of teaching. What does a grade mean? It should reflect a student's overall response to the totality of learning activities in the work being graded—not just his response to an isolated test, but to his participation in class, to all parts of the work. It is regrettable that grades are so often only symbols of victory or failure in a competition. The race horse gets an *A* because something in his genes made him a race horse, and the plow horse doesn't get above a *C* because circumstances over which he has no control made him a plow horse. Is that fair? Is it just? Though administrators may argue—citing college entrance standards or future employers' wishes as their chief justification—that no plow horse should ever receive a mark above *C*, suppose that the plow horse is running the very best race he can. Must he be penalized because God didn't give him the quickness of Man o' War? Maybe God would argue that if a penalty is in order, it should be assessed against God himself.

What we are saying is that schoolwork should be conceived and evaluation should be interpreted in such a way that anybody who makes an effort can enjoy the sweet smell of success. Even a slow learner who works as hard and as diligently as he can should not face locked doors labeled *A* and *B*. Nor should the fast learner have all doors automatically open to him only because he is a fast learner.

Evaluation, in English and in other subjects, has long been the least humane thing that we teachers do. In this volume, we have stressed constantly the need for humaneness, the need for concern with the student as an individual, the encouragement of growth rather than the relegation of any student to a permanent classification. What is done with evaluation is, or can be, one of the most significant aspects of humaneness.

Appendix A
Personnel

SOUTHERN ILLINOIS UNIVERSITY: William H. Evans,
Ellen A. Frogner, Roy Weshinskey
UNIVERSITY OF CHICAGO: Janet A. Emig,
Gwin J. Kolb, James F. McCampbell, Robert Parker
UNIVERSITY OF ILLINOIS: Raymond D. Crisp,
William H. Evans, J. N. Hook, Paul H. Jacobs,
Alan L. Madsen
WESTERN ILLINOIS UNIVERSITY: Thomas N. Filson,
Alfred Lindsey, Jr., Sherman Rush

THE ISCPET ADVISORY COMMITTEE

Harry S. Broudy, University of Illinois
Dwight L. Burton, Florida State University
W. Nelson Francis, Brown University
Nathaniel Gage, Stanford University
Alfred H. Grommon, Stanford University
Clarence W. Hach, Evanston Township High School
William Riley Parker, Indiana University (deceased)
Robert C. Pooley, Madison, Wisconsin
Loren Reid, University of Missouri
William D. Sheldon, Syracuse University
James R. Squire, former Executive Secretary, NCTE
Donald R. Tuttle, U.S. Office of Education

AD HOC COMMITTEES WITHIN THE TWENTY COOPERATING INSTITUTIONS

(a total of nearly two hundred persons)

EXECUTIVE COMMITTEE OF ISCPET

Raymond D. Crisp, University of Illinois
(nonvoting), 1966–69
William H. Evans, University of Illinois and
Southern Illinois University, 1964–66
John S. Gerrietts, Loyola University, 1964–66;
chairman, 1965–66
John M. Heissler, Illinois State University, 1966–69;
chairman, 1967–68
J. N. Hook, University of Illinois, 1964–69
Paul H. Jacobs, University of Illinois, 1964–69
(nonvoting, 1964–66)

Alfred L. Papillon, DePaul University, 1967–69;
chairman, 1968–69
Justus R. Pearson, Illinois Wesleyan University, 1967–68;
chairman, 1964–65
Roy K. Weshinskey, Southern Illinois University, 1964–69;
chairman, 1966–67

SPEAKERS AND CONSULTANTS AT ISCPET'S SEMIANNUAL MEETINGS

(exclusive of Advisory Committee members)

Roger K. Applebee, University of Illinois
Bruce Appleby, Southern Illinois University
Joseph Beaver, Northeastern Illinois State University
Ellen Brachtl, District Superintendent,
Chicago Public Schools
Sue M. Brett, U.S. Office of Education
Robert L. Brissenden, Illinois State Certification Board
Evelyn Carlson, Associate Superintendent,
Chicago Public Schools
Sister Mary Philippa Coogan, Carmel High School,
Mundelein
Margaret Crow, Carbondale High School
Florence Dahlberg, Monmouth High School
Arthur M. Eastman, Carnegie-Mellon University
Edmund L. Epstein, Southern Illinois University
Judith Feinberg, Schurz High School, Chicago
Louanna Furbee, Illinois Institute of Technology
Norman Gronlund, University of Illinois
Harold L. Herber, Syracuse University
George V. Herman, Deerfield High School
Ruth Hoffmeyer, Chicago Public Schools
Ryoji Inoue, Nagoya, Japan
Arno Jewett, U.S. Office of Education
Esmor Jones, National Association for the Teaching of
English (England)
Warren Jones, Englewood High School, Chicago
Robert E. Lewis, Wendell Phillips High School, Chicago
Andrew MacLeish, University of Minnesota
Samuel T. Mayo, Loyola University
Dennis Moore, Northwestern University
Aldo Mungai, Lyons Township High School, La Grange

Emily Pettigrew, Illinois Institute of Technology
Robert C. Pooley, Madison, Wisconsin
Helen Rademacher, Edison Junior High School, Champaign
Sister M. Aloisa Rossiter, St. Benedict High School, Chicago
Elizabeth Rusk, Michigan State University
J. T. Sandefur, Kansas State Teachers College, Emporia
Michael Shugrue, Modern Language Association of America
Helmuth J. Simon, Tel Aviv, Israel
Marjorie Smiley, Hunter College of the City University of New York
Robert Stake, University of Illinois
John Sullivan, Chicago Public Schools
Robert Sutton, University of Illinois
Priscilla Tyler, University of Missouri, Kansas City
Katherine Visovatti, Elk Grove Research and Development Center
Ronald L. Wardhaugh, University of Michigan
Stuart Wilson, State University of New York, Fredonia

HEADQUARTERS STAFF

Helen A. Bohlen, Secretary, 1968–69
Raymond D. Crisp, Research Associate, 1966–69
William H. Evans, Associate Director, 1964–66
Jean Ewing, Secretary, 1966–67
J. N. Hook, Director, 1964–69
Paul H. Jacobs, Research Associate, 1964–66;
    Associate Director, 1966–69
Charlene Myers, Secretary, 1964–66
Deloris P. Jones, Clerical Assistant, 1967–69
Mary van den Bergh, Secretary, 1967–68
Esther H. Webber, Secretary, 1968–69

Appendix B

Studies

The Special Research Studies of the
Illinois State-Wide Curriculum Study Center in the Preparation
of Secondary School Teachers of English

Details on any of these studies may be obtained from their directors. The annotations are brief descriptions, not titles.

AURORA COLLEGE. A study of a special two-semester internship program involving prospective secondary English teachers as assistants in the teaching of college freshman English classes. The assumption being tested here is that prospective English teachers with this type of pre-internship experience will perform better during their regular internship and, also, after they enter the profession. (Directed by Professor Ethel W. Tapper.)

BRADLEY UNIVERSITY. a. Cooperative study of literature programs (coordinated by North Central College). (Originally directed by Professor William L. Gillis; completed by Mrs. June Snider.)

b. A study to determine the validity of a minimal composition program for students entering a career of English teaching, if the students study composition at the optimum time. (Originally directed by Professor William L. Gillis; completed by Mrs. June Snider.)

c. A study to determine which of three or which combination of three courses in the methodology of teaching English is most effective. (Originally directed by Professor William L. Gillis; completed by Mrs. June Snider.)

d. A fact-finding survey of the present status of the teaching of English in grades 10, 11, and 12 of Illinois schools. (Directed by Professor William L. Gillis.)

DE PAUL UNIVERSITY. A study involving development, teaching, and evaluation of the results of a course in advanced English composition, designed especially for prospective teachers of secondary English. (Directed by Professors Margaret M. Neville and Alfred L. Papillon.)

GREENVILLE COLLEGE. A nationwide study of the supervision of student teaching in English. (Directed by Professor Donald Pennington.)

ILLINOIS INSTITUTE OF TECHNOLOGY. a. A study to prepare materials (syllabus, bibliography, and illustrative tape recordings) for a course in social problems in the English language. (Directed by Professor A. L. Davis.)

b. Recordings of standard English in the United States and Canada. (Directed by Professor A. L. Davis.)

ILLINOIS STATE UNIVERSITY. A fact-finding survey of the teaching of English in grades 7, 8, and 9 of Illinois schools. (Directed by Professor John M. Heissler.)

ILLINOIS WESLEYAN UNIVERSITY. a. Cooperative study of literature programs (coordinated by North Central College). (Directed by Professor Justus R. Pearson.)

b. A study involving examination and evaluation of traditional and contemporary English grammars being taught in selected colleges and universities across the country, and establishment and evaluation of courses in language suitable for prospective teachers of secondary English. (Directed by Professor Justus R. Pearson, Illinois Wesleyan University, and Professor James R. Reese, now at East Tennessee State University.)

KNOX COLLEGE. a. A study involving a transformational grammar inservice seminar, the development of general guidelines for teaching a unit on transformational grammar in the high school, and the development of videotapes to be used as teaching aids for prospective and inservice teachers of English. (Directed by Professor Michael G. Crowell.) b. The preparation of videotapes and kinescopes and the use of them in the training of prospective secondary English teachers. (Directed by Professor Carl Eisemann.)

LOYOLA UNIVERSITY. a. Cooperative study of literature programs (coordinated by North Central College). (Directed by Professor Rita Clarkson.)

b. A study involving development, teaching, and evaluation of a secondary English methods course, with the major emphasis being on the development of critical thinking skills on the part of prospective English teachers. (Directed by Sister Mary Constantine, S.S.J.)

c. A study of the effects of a speech unit and a unit in the art of questioning, designed especially for prospective secondary English teachers in a student teaching course, upon their performance in secondary English instruction. (Directed by Sister Mary Constantine, S.S.J.)

d. A study of the effects upon experienced English teachers, without previous training in student teaching, of a five-hour course entitled "Student Teaching" and involving emphasis upon critical thinking in teaching. (Directed by Sister Mary Constantine, S.S.J.)

e. A study of the value of courses in the classics ("The Classical Epic"; "The Classical Theater"), offered as electives, in the curriculum of prospective high school teachers of English. (Directed by Professor Joseph Wolff.)

MONMOUTH COLLEGE. a. A study to determine the desirability of instruction in oral interpretation of literature in the preparation of prospective secondary school teachers of English. (Directed by Professor Thomas L. Fernandez.)

b. A study to develop a course in oral interpretation designed to meet the professional needs of prospective secondary school teachers of English. (Directed by Professor Thomas L. Fernandez.)

NORTH CENTRAL COLLEGE. a. An evaluation of the effectiveness of an earlier reorganization of the teacher training curriculum. (Directed by Professor Erling Peterson.)

b. Coordination of a cooperative study to evaluate the relative effectiveness of five different approaches to the teaching of literature in college: by genre, by groups of literary types, by core plus some basic categories, by intensive textual study with a highly structured historical framework, or by diversified period. (Directed by Professor Erling Peterson.)

NORTHWESTERN UNIVERSITY. A study of the effectiveness of a filmed training program in composition for in-service teachers as an agent of change in the secondary school. (Directed by Professors Wallace Douglas and Stephen Judy.)

OLIVET NAZARENE COLLEGE. A comprehensive study of the personal and academic qualifications essential to the successful teaching of the slow learner in high school English, and the structuring or modifying of the curriculum for the preparation of teachers, embodying elements of training found desirable. (Directed by Professor Lottie Phillips.)

ROOSEVELT UNIVERSITY. A comparison of the teaching practices of teachers with and without formal preparation in linguistics. (Directed by Professors William Makely and William Leppert.)

ST. XAVIER COLLEGE. A study to determine what high school English teachers conceive their role to be in the teaching of reading; the amount and kinds of preparation they have had for that role; and the current status of reading instruction in the secondary school English classroom. (Directed by Professor George McGuire.)

SOUTHERN ILLINOIS UNIVERSITY. a. Development of an opinionnaire concerned with particular areas of language and an analysis of the returns from administering the opinionnaire to prospective English teachers and teachers in service. (Directed by Professor Ellen A. Frogner, Edwardsville campus.)

b. Development, administration, and analysis of examinations based on the ISCPET "Qualifications of Secondary School Teachers of English: A Preliminary Statement" (cosponsored by the University of Illinois). (Directed by Professor William H. Evans, Southern Illinois University, Carbondale campus, and Professor Paul H. Jacobs, University of Illinois.)

UNIVERSITY OF CHICAGO. a. Master of arts in the teaching of English programs: a directory. (Directed by Professors Janet A. Emig and James F. McCampbell.)

b. A comparative study of two master of arts in the teaching of English (MATE) programs in Illinois. (Directed by Professors Janet A. Emig and James F. McCampbell.)

UNIVERSITY OF ILLINOIS. a. See the second study for Southern Illinois University.

b. Cooperative study of literature programs (coordinated by North Central College). (Directed by Professor Paul H. Jacobs.)

c. A study to determine the level of competence in educational measurement and evaluation possessed by Illinois secondary English teachers now in service and to ascertain the level of competence desirable in prospective English teachers. (Directed by Professor Paul H. Jacobs and Research Associate Raymond D. Crisp.)

d. A study to describe knowledge of concepts from literary criticism, its types and methods of approach to literature, possessed by prospective secondary school teachers of English who are presently enrolled in courses in methods of teaching secondary school English at ISCPET institutions. (Directed by Professor Alan Madsen.)

e. A study to determine how experienced secondary school English teachers in Illinois rate themselves in areas of knowledge of English and knowledge and skill in teaching English. The study also seeks to determine if there is a significant relationship between those self-evaluations and the number of years of teaching experience and the college degrees held by the teachers. (Directed by Research Associate Raymond D. Crisp.)

WESTERN ILLINOIS UNIVERSITY. a. A study involving development, teaching, and evaluation of the results of a course for teachers in service devoted to the practical application of linguistics, of principles of composition, and of various approaches to the teaching of the slow learner. (Directed by Professor Alfred Lindsey, Jr., Western Illinois University, and Professor Thomas N. Filson, now of the University of Michigan.)

b. A study to determine the effect on teacher attitude and performance of an inservice, university extension program of professional readings for secondary school English teachers who do not have a major in English and who teach in small Illinois public high schools. (Directed by Professor Alfred Lindsey, Jr.)